T0208789

PSYCHOLOGY WITH A
SPARKLE

DR. DENISE O'DWYER

ARCHWAY
PUBLISHING

Archway Publishing books may be ordered through booksellers or by contacting:

Archway Publishing
1663 Liberty Drive
Bloomington, IN 47403
www.archwaypublishing.com
844-669-3957

Because of the dynamic nature of the Internet, any web addresses or links contained in this book may have changed since publication and may no longer be valid. The views expressed in this work are solely those of the author and do not necessarily reflect the views of the publisher, and the publisher hereby disclaims any responsibility for them.

Interior Graphics/Art Credit: Hugh Sweeney,
Filmmaker, Photographer & Videographer

Any scripture quotations are from the ESV® Bible (The Holy Bible, English Standard Version®), Copyright © 2001 by Crossway, a publishing ministry of Good News Publishers. Used by permission. All rights reserved.

ISBN: 978-1-6657-3152-2 (sc)
ISBN: 978-1-6657-3151-5 (hc)
ISBN: 978-1-6657-3159-1 (e)

Library of Congress Control Number: 2022914494

Print information available on the last page.

Archway Publishing rev. date: 10/14/2022

DEDICATION

To my amazing and resilient Mum, who inspires me every day to live life with our greatest effort, and with kindness and grace; and to my firecracker Dad, who has colourfully inspired this journey in spirit with me, each step of the way. xx D.

"She was unstoppable, not because she did not have failures or doubts, but because she continued on despite them."
– unknown

PREFACE

It is said that change happens when the fear of remaining tight in a bud is more painful than the risk it takes to blossom. This book has taken physical form based on years of studying, researching, practicing, listening, observing, reading, reflecting, evaluating and re-evaluating all things Psychology, Human Consciousness, and Personal Development related. The content has been variously influenced by a smorgasbord of insightful people who have captured my imagination over the years, including psychologists, writers, artists, activists, entrepreneurs, fashion designers, poets, physicians, healers, leaders, psychics, mystics, spiritual warriors, athletes, architects, musicians, actors, presenters, comedians, colleagues, friends, family, followers, and not least of all my wonderful clients. My hope in writing this book, is to inspire and assist the everyday person with everyday life, fostering hope and encouragement to break free from fears and limited belief systems which unduly harass, slow, and halt human development.

INTENTION

I believe our ability to assist and connect with people from all walks of life in an informed, meaningful way, is only as good as our willingness to acknowledge our shared humanity, struggles, and ongoing areas of personal development. Our ability to communicate this in a relatable, non-elitist manner more readily captures the imagination of a diverse population, and to this end, I have incorporated key examples from my personal and professional life, to highlight particular areas and life lessons from which I have struggled, overcome, and continue to grow each day. This is to illustrate that although professionally trained in the scientific study of human behaviour …..this does not preclude Psychologists or indeed any other, from being faced with the inevitable peaks, struggles, flatlines and triumphs of everyday life.

INTRODUCTION

Recent years have observed a definite paradigm shift in global con-sciousness, with corresponding changes in the evolving human land-scape. People are reflecting more, questioning more, evaluating more, expressing more, and opening their hearts and minds to a broader kind of holistic intelligence. Antiquated thought and belief systems which focus singularly on pharmacological solutions are being stress tested for proof of functional validity and reliability, as people look beyond the lens of limitation and disease, and the hierarchical power structures which have supported this paradigm. A new age of transparency, authenticity, co-authorship, co-production, compassion, renewal and regeneration is emerging, and I'm excited to contribute to this luminary new wave!

Our individual and collective psychology impacts everything – from how we respond to the subjectively sublime, to the perceived shameful. How we think, how we feel, how we behave, and ultimately how we respond to life, have roots in how we experienced the world as children - our early environment, our trauma related histories, and our then available support systems. Together, these have an impressive bearing on how we show up in the world as adults, and by examining our adopted maladaptive thinking and behaviour patterns, taking the appropriate responsibility rather than blame-shifting, we better equip and empower ourselves to change and become as we would wish.

Psychology with a Sparkle is a contemporary summary of thoughts, ideas, insights, research and reflections - many of which regularly present for people, both in and outside of formal therapy. It offers a light-hearted journey of professional insights, personal stories, scientific research, and tips and strategies for dealing with the seemingly fixed and immovable, to sparkling fluidity. An informal style makes this pocket book accessible to everyone, and although the chapters may better flow when approached in sequence, read in the manner you feel most inspired…

Welcome to Psychology with a Sparkle!

CHAPTER OUTLINE

FEEL THE FEAR AND DO IT ANYWAY

In writing this book, I've had several million moments of wanting it to be finished, yet resisting the actual discipline of sitting down and committing words to a page. It wasn't until March 2020, when I, like everyone else was forced into lockdown due to Covid-19, that I truly found my writer's rhythm. I work as a Principal Psychologist for a large organisation in Ireland - who like many others, tailored their services to accommodate and support people remotely throughout the pandemic. At a time when there was little happening by way of social events - no hanging out with friends, no gigs, traveling, holidays; no attending parties, matches, restaurants, bars, gyms, leisure centres...but we could go for a run within five kilometres of our homes! – I figured it was now or never!

Book Inception

Writing a book has always been on my bucket list. I had captioned the title, dreamed the content, visualised the cover, written the chapter outlines - yet still hadn't fully committed words to a page. I came up with the usual excuses – "It's not the right time" or "I don't have enough time" - yet ironically, still found the time to scroll Instagram and read countless books and content written by others! This is a classic example of wanting the end result, yet sabotaging the all-important climb to the summit.

As humans, we're often expert in this field - keen on the fantasy or manifestation of the goal or dream, though less committed to the actual action steps involved in getting there. We delude ourselves that by simply consuming others' content - by watching a motivational YouTube video, listening to trending podcasts and reading countless books, we'll become magically imbued with similar qualities. Whilst reading, listening and observing others' content is certainly useful from the perspective of deepening our insight, awareness, knowledge and understanding, it remains a largely time-wasting activity if the information ingested fails to inspire any meaningful action.

In my case, it took quite a journey before I stopped looking outside of myself and began to trust my own wisdom and inner guidance system. I had somehow convinced myself that what others had to say was probably of more value or interest, and this faulty thinking kept me locked in a state of fear and immobilisation for much too long. I watched and admired as those in similar or related fields, made their mark - seemingly with ease and confidence, and although I had glimpses of personal potential: external moments of encouragement and validation, followed by quiet moments of reflection, I struggled to raise my head fully above the parapet.

I completed my Doctoral research in 2016 in the area of wellbeing and mental health, and this was received with an unprecedented wave of enthusiasm on the pre-COVID international conference front. I had thus completed the research, studied the academic papers, read the books, listened to the podcasts, watched the Ted Talks and immersed myself in the all-important journaling, therapeutic and self-development work - activities which I continue to this day. Yet I still didn't quite trust myself to say what I wanted to say in the right way – whatever that is!

Blind Courage

Osho proposed that courage is a love affair with the unknown, which has pretty much been my writing experience throughout. Some days were filled with passion and promise whilst others left me drowning in a sea of bewilderment and self-doubt. Despite encouragement from others, fear makes us second guess our skills, talents and abilities - often making us anxious, self-conscious (Wagner & Morisi, 2019) and introverted and shy (Keighin et al. 2009). Left unchecked, this can reduce us to a state of analysis-paralysis and resulting inaction, for which the only antidote is to take immediate courageous action. "Do it scared", giving no power to the internal critic or external be-grudgers and naysayers.

When we enable the internal or external negative committee to take hold and dictate how we think and behave, we're doomed to an imprisoned life of fear, limitation and an unhealthy narcissistic, inward focus. In the grips of such, we never fully realise our true potential - nor do we get to share it with others. As some of the most successful leaders throughout the world attest, - there is no such thing as being fearless 100% of the time, but there is such a thing as powering through in spite of the fear.

> **"No one is you and that is your power"**
> **– Dave Grohl**

Holding ourselves accountable, acknowledging our strengths and weak-nesses, taking ourselves to task, and changing the narrative on the ob-solete stories we repeatedly tell ourselves - are I believe, some of the cornerstones to achieving personal and professional happiness, of which success is a natural by-product. By activating our personal potential, we not only equip ourselves to achieve and maximise our gifts, we also contribute to the greater good of humanity.

Thus, when operating in a flow state at full capacity, using our God-given talents and abilities - the world considerably benefits, as do we. Since there is no other person on this earth quite like you, with your unique set of gifts, skills and talents – they will remain forever obscured and denied to the world, if you fail to value and take pride in what you have to offer. Viewed from this perspective, executing and following through on our goals and desires is a heart-centred mission, as opposed to being ego-centred. What better reason to celebrate and share our gifts with the world!

The Science Piece - Summary of my Research on Mental Health and Wellbeing

The empirical evidence from my 2015 Doctoral research part-inspired this book. It examined Wellness Recovery Action Planning (WRAP) as a system for managing the mental health and wellbeing of people with mental health difficulties and also as a potential system for people who had suffered an acquired brain Injury (ABI).

Wellness Recovery Action Planning (WRAP) had its initial inception in the U.S., where the Founder, Mary Ellen Copeland, introduced this peer supported, personalised approach to wellness and recovery (Copeland, 1997). Born out of and rooted in the principles of self-determination, WRAP helps people to:

1) Decrease and prevent intrusive or troubling feelings and behaviours
2) Increase personal empowerment;
3) Improve quality of life
4) Achieve their own life goals and dreams

– copelandcentre.com

WRAP Research Summary

In summary, my research employed quantitative design to measure the effectiveness of introducing a weekly Wellness Recovery Action Plan (WRAP) intervention to reduce the anxiety and depression levels of people with mental health diagnoses (MH) and those with an acquired brain injury (ABI). By introducing WRAP into their daily lives, participants were given a structure to manage and improve their mental health and wellbeing.

The WRAP intervention was comprised of eight weekly psycho-educational sessions in the case of the Mental Health cohort, and twelve weekly sessions in the case of the ABI cohort, where clients discussed and created personal notes pertaining to the following:

- Daily tools and strategies for maintaining wellbeing
- Identification of internal and external triggers
- Recognition of early warning signs of mental, physical, psychological and emotional distress and deterioration
- Ameliorating crises through advance planning and self-care.
- Post-crisis planning

In addition to working through the core weekly WRAP program as summarised above, concepts such as radical acceptance, mindfulness, thought redirection, breathing techniques and grounding exercises were included, to enhance the experience of participants and offer practical coping strategies for use across settings.

The results of the research were highly significant for each of the groups that took part in the WRAP intervention - mental health (MH) and acquired brain injury (ABI), as compared with their control group counterparts, i.e. those who were on a waiting list to participate at a later time in the WRAP intervention.

Due to memory and attention difficulties, a few tweaks were necessary in the case of the ABI group. These related to questionnaire design and reinforcement of material over a longer duration (twelve weeks instead of eight). However, the results overall demonstrated significant reductions in the anxiety and depression levels for both participating cohorts. (Appendix 1)

Consciousness Rising

In analysing the results of my research, it was empirically as well as perceptually evident, that the expectations of people and social climate to mental health and disability had changed. A new paradigm of holistic wellbeing and recovery was steadily emerging, replacing the formerly limiting view of mental health through the lens of disease and pharmacological solutions only. There was an eagerness for people to explore and examine the accommodations necessary to become their own recovery protagonists, and based on the results of my study, WRAP was proving a worthy contender for this purpose.

What is WRAP?

WRAP or Wellness Recovery Action Planning (Copeland, 1997) offers participants a functional, transferrable, measurable and accessible system toward navigating their personal well-being path. Many who participated in my research, reported enjoying the empowering, bespoke approach it offered, enabling participants to themselves identify what was uniquely helpful in supporting their daily well-being and recovery, as opposed to being prescriptively told what to do. In addition to weekly group WRAP sessions, participants were encouraged to maintain contact with their relevant health-care professionals and to continue with their respective treatment options, whilst utilising WRAP as an adjunct complementary recovery tool.

My research was received very favourably on the global, 2018/2019 pre-COVID front, which I suspect was partially to do with the novel nature of the WRAP intervention, as well as the statistical significance of the results for both cohorts – mental health and ABI. Anxiety and depression are among the secondary mental health difficulties observed post-ABI (Mallaya et al, 2015; Eriksson et al, 2009) and WRAP demonstrated a functional approach for dealing with such secondary difficulties. In conducting my research, there appeared to be no evidence of WRAP having been previously trialled with an ABI population - which in this study, proved highly significant.

Imposter Syndrome

Whilst presenting my research at various conferences internationally, I was led to question why among other things, we are often quick to commend the knowledge, expertise and skills of others, yet slower to trust or value our own? Indeed research has supported this claim, indicating that those who possess the most self-awareness generally underestimate their ability, whereas those who perceive themselves as being highly self-aware, demonstrate the least amount of self-awareness (Eurich, 2018).

To coin the words of Charles Bukowski, "The problem with the world is that fools and fanatics are always so certain of themselves, yet wiser people are full of doubts." The modern day term for this is 'Imposter Syndrome' - a widely held term for feeling unqualified or unworthy despite evidence to the contrary. Guess that makes me an imposter then - in daily recovery!

Overcoming Imposter Syndrome

Some years ago, I attended a Personal Development Conference in Italy, delivered by internationally renowned Motivational Coach, Author and Speaker, Anthony Robbins. This formidable giant of a man, who has impacted in excess of fifty million lives across the world, is an energy to behold. One of my abiding recollections of this four-day marathon event (apart from walking barefoot across hot coals, and meeting an equally hot Italian guy!), was Robbins telling the audience that regardless of who he has mentored across the world – from celebrities to entrepreneurs, millionaires to billionaires, and everything in-between - regardless of their background, education, knowledge, culture, status or success - the underlying belief held most commonly by humans is, "Am I enough?" "Does what I do matter?"

Oprah has similarly alluded to this frequently emerging theme among the many big stars and celebrity guests she has interviewed over the years – who regularly look to her at the end of their interview for reassurance, that they have indeed, done a good job.

The belief that everyone else is doing exponentially better, and somehow have their lives more impressively figured out than we ourselves, can significantly hinder the human experience - leading to all kinds of unhelpful thoughts and emotions. Lack of self-belief or Imposter Syndrome as it's commonly known, is something we all share to some degree - although the internal voice of the imposter is more amplified for some than for others. Common concerns arising for people, include their skills, talents, ability, intelligence, worthiness, wittiness, attractiveness, youthfulness, maturity, sexiness, ability to receive and experience pleasure, happiness, joy, success, health, prosperity, promotion, connection, belonging and love.

As humans, we have a deep need to connect with others - to feel acknowledged, valued, understood, respected and loved. We want to believe that what we do somehow matters and makes a difference in the world and in the lives of others, yet so often feelings of inadequacy plague the human mind - compromising or inhibiting forward progression. Concerns may become so heightened to the point of complete avoidance, inaction or self-sabotage. This occurs where an individual engages in safety seeking behaviours to avoid the feelings of anxiety and inadequacy associated with the experience of exposing oneself to a particular triggering situation.

For example: Staying indoors to escape the anxiety associated with meeting people; dodging a presentation because of fear of public speaking; not voicing an opinion for fear of judgment; not asking someone out to avoid rejection; not starting a project for fear of not finishing it; not attending a party due to social anxiety; not attempting something new due fear of not being immediately good at it; not posting on social media for fear of not receiving enough likes/views. The list prevails. Whilst inaction may temporarily abate feelings of fear or anxiety - remaining mute, not taking action and never truly expressing our unique fingerprint in the world - is rarely if ever a satisfying or lasting solution. To quote Elbert Hubbard, "To avoid criticism, do nothing, say nothing, be nothing."

Chance meetings or aligned encounters?

The final motivation for completing this book occurred in July 2018, when I presented my WRAP wellbeing research at a Neuropsychology Conference in Prague. I was introduced by a colleague and friend to the Senior Editor of a U.K. Academic Publishing House, which facilitated a discussion emerging about my research, and my interest in writing a book along similar themes. After chatting briefly, the Editor took my details, advising she was soon to arrive at another conference in Galway, and was interested in meeting to further discuss. Although sceptical that anything might ever come of this, I felt immensely grateful and super-excited for having met someone truly lovely from the world of publishing - I saw it as an encouraging wink from the universe!

Some weeks later, I followed up and was thrilled to receive an email from the Editor confirming her arrival in Galway. We agreed a meeting time and place, and as requested, I brought along my manuscript outline. With take-away coffees in hand, we sat over-looking Galway Bay, where a combination of sea air and wild Atlantic wind provided just the right calming influence for my adrenaline-charged body and mind. As the Editor meticulously scrolled through my notes, I used just about every super-power I had to remain calm and grounded. Finally, in what felt like several million lifetimes - she lifted her head, and excitedly beamed, "Yes! I think we have something here!"

Was this actually happening? Was I being considered for a traditional book deal, as a first-time author? This was a genuine pinch-me moment, one which I'll never forget! The Editor explained how things would proceed from this point – I was required to send a formal detailed proposal of my manuscript to the Publishers. This would then be reviewed by the internal editorial board, before being sent out for external review.

Head, Heart and Gut Instinct

I completed and returned the proposal as requested - setting the intention that my submission would be received with open minds and hearts.

#DrDee

In true universal law style, I then relinquished my attachment to the outcome and carried on with everyday life. Three months passed when I spotted amidst a sea of emails, the subject heading, "Book Proposal". My heart skipped a beat as I clicked to open. There it was……..the proposal…..my proposal. MY DEBUT PROPOSAL WAS ACCEPTED!!! The opening lines literally jumped off the screen. After suitably composing myself, I read further to discover the fine print which outlined two stipulations. As Academic Publishers offering a traditional book deal, the acceptance criteria required me to change the title of my work, and to include more empirical research.

Recognising the enormity of being offered a traditional book deal with such esteemed publishers, as an unknown debut author - I took due consideration in making what felt like a ginormous decision! I discussed the offer with a selected few - and as always, immersed myself in reflection, journaling, meditation and prayer to inform my best decision. Whilst some felt that a first time publication with established academic publishers was absolutely the way to go, others remarked, "If you take the sparkle out of it, you'll take yourself out of it"; "The sparkle is what gives it the sparkle, and if you remove that, you'll remove yourself, and the very essence of what makes the book different."

Follow your Gut but take your Brain with you!

As a professional Psychologist, I'm accustomed to the practice of undertaking and publishing relevant research - which is formative to good decision making and best practice, as well as being instrumental to increasing the scientific database of knowledge for the wider collective. I'm also somewhat of a mystic at heart however, who looks for signs and believes in the power of instinct and intuition! I believe that both science and intuition operate as complementary, component tools, which can serve to guide and inform best practice.

In this particular incidence, whilst logically and analytically, my mind was telling me to proceed via the traditional academic publishing route - my instinct was guiding me in an altogether different direction.

I believed the book title I had chosen, gave it a unique, modern edge, and having studied the analytics of my social media platforms, I was aware that content receiving the most engagement, was that which was presented in a contemporary, relatable manner - combining professional and personal insight, as opposed to being overly dominated by statistics and figures - as per traditional psychological research. The decision from my perspective was therefore less to do with the further inclusion of objective research, and more with allowing me the freedom to retain my book title - which I believed facilitated the expression of a less formal, less conformist, more modern style.

Feel the Fear and Do it Anyway

Fears and doubts about how the book might be received held me in a state of analysis-paralysis for longer than necessary. Was my choice to write in a more creative manner the right one? Would I be harshly judged for choosing to go outside traditional Psychology parameters? Was I right to decline the initial offer of being published with traditional academic publishers? Would I serve people with my eclectic mix of experience, reflections, scientific research and personal anecdotes as effectively, as compared to providing a steady stream of statistics and empirical re-search? Fear of showing up in my preferred style, kept me locked in a procrastination-perfectionist loop for much too long. The voice of ego screamed fear, insecurity and an instruction to remain tightly within known parameters, whilst my intuition offered an encouraging nudge of courage, liberation, excitement and sparkle!

American Author and Professor of Literature, Joseph Campbell, suggested, "What will they think of me, must be put aside for bliss." Thus, I began my non-fiction journey, reminding myself each time fear attempted to take hold, "You'll never be everyone's cup of tea, but you may just be someone's shot of whiskey!" Deep down, I had faith that as a completed work, my book would find its intended audience, who would benefit from whatever information I felt inspired to share. The more freely I could pen my words, the more potency I believed the book would have as a completed work.

THE SECRET TO
SUCCESS IS FOUND IN
THE DAILY ROUND

Defining Success in the 21st Century

Depending upon our unique psychology, disposition and perspective, success looks different for everyone. For someone recovering from a serious life-threatening illness or accident, success may be the wondrous gift of opening their eyes and breathing new life. For another, in the prime of their health, success may include a thriving career, attractive partner, toned bod, smoking sex life, frequent luxury vacations, mass popularity, millions in the bank and an impressive Insta following - all at the same time #obvs! I jest. Although we have many stereotyped impressions of what success looks like on the surface, it is our responsibility to define what it means to each of us individually and how it relates to our personal values.

> **"Someone who is healthy has a million dreams.
> Someone who is not, has one" (unknown)**

Success Impactors

Social Media gets a bad wrap for perpetuating the seemingly competitive, narcissistic, instant success oriented culture often observed, and whilst social media may well be a contributing factor, it doesn't merit sole responsibility. Entrepreneur and Social Media Mogul, Gary Vee proposes, "Social media is not responsible for making people develop entitled attitudes, it has simply heightened people's predispositions to becoming that way"(Vaynerchuk, 2020). In other words, if someone has a pre-morbid attitude of entitlement, social media merely exacerbates this tendency.

Biology, genes and epigenetics have historically been considered the root cause for pretty much everything (Bush, 2022; Murphy, 2020; Leaf, 2015) however we now know there are very often other mitigating factors when it comes to understanding human psychology and behaviour. Perhaps the reason therefore for heightened expectations and/or a grandiose attitude may be more accurately rooted in a myriad of factors - including genes and biology, early childhood experiences, psychological, environmental, educational, social, emotional and digital impactors.

We each hold personal responsibility for who and what we choose to follow – whether online or in real life. Where we place our attention largely impacts who and what we become, and whilst there's nothing wrong with being influenced by others or aspiring to a seemingly better life, problems may arise if people's perspectives or value systems become so apparently out of whack with reality – with little value placed on anything other than the external, aesthetic or material representations of success.

Colouring outside the lines

Viewing things from a unidimensional perspective, can be the result of following the same types of accounts in the online space, or exposing oneself to the same kinds of people in the external world. This results in an echo chamber or 'confirmation bias', as coined by Psychologist, Peter Wason (1960), where people's beliefs and opinions are insulated from rebuttal due to the closed, confined system of which they remain a part. This amplifies and reinforces the acceptance of information which confirms or strengthens one's own beliefs, values or opinions, however it does little by way of expanding thought or creativity. This invariably leads to a more narcissistic focus, with less tolerance for opposing or differing views, and difficulty connecting with anything other than positive, agreeable emotions - similar to one's own.

Living Inspired

Psychologist and Author, Dr. Rick Hanson proposes we move from states to traits (Hanson, 2012). In other words, if we find ourselves being solely consumed with the worldly and material "states" or representations of success, e.g. our financial state, our property and possessions, our appearance, social media following etc., we might instead consider cultivating the less immediately obvious representations or traits of success, e.g. honesty, respect, compassion, kindness, humour, inclusivity, diversity, empathy, security, confidence, integrity, freedom, growth. Trinity College Dublin, Psychology Professor, Ian Robertson, similarly encourages the cultivation of 'authentic success', as distinct from the temporary, more vacant expressions of the term (Robertson, 2021).

It is up to each of us to individually define our personal definition of success, which may include any or all of the above success markers. Our definition of success is likely to change over time, depending on various life experiences, and whilst there's nothing wrong with desiring or enjoying the occasionally fun, frivolous, extravagant or fashionable – at least I hope so! Our definition of success is better stretched to include a more authentic, holistic and lasting perspective.

The Consumption Effect

Dr. Joe Dispenza, known for his profound work on how to discover the full potential of the human brain, proposes that our personality is what creates our personal reality and if, as he purports, our personality is made up of how we think, how we feel and how we act - then what we consume on a daily basis has a huge bearing on our mental representation of success (Dispenza, 2022). Internal and external influences make up our environment and include; the thoughts we think, the people with whom we surround ourselves, our diet, exercise habits, our work, relationships, hobbies, intellectual stimulation and online consumption. These are among the many impactors which affect both our input and output each day, so it's important we get clear on the effect of each in contributing or inhibiting the personal success we desire.

Rise and Sparkle

According to the research of Dr. Fred Luskin of Stanford University; a human being has approximately 60, 000 thoughts per day, 90% of which are repetitive (Rickman, 2012). Is it any wonder therefore, how our lives often reflect sameness or lack of creativity and progression, if we're unwilling to challenge the antiquated thought and belief systems which very often keep us locked in daily maladaptive thinking and behaviour patterns. As the quote - often misattributed to Mark Twain among famous others, states, "The definition of insanity is doing the same thing over and over and expecting different results." We are creatures of habit, so the comfortable option is often to ignore internal impulses, and continue doing what's familiar. Evolution and progress require us to change however, and change requires discipline, consistency and levelling up with who we are, and where we're at in our lives.

Most people, consciously or otherwise, know they are capable of infinitely more. Like most things calling for our attention, any impulse for change generally starts as a gentle nudge from within. If ignored, the impulse becomes louder and more aggressive and if repeatedly ignored, it can show up in our physical bodies as pain or physical illness (Cassel, 2017). Similarly, if we find ourselves in a persistent heightened or reactive states, this may indicate more deep rooted emotional issues which have been buried, ignored or suppressed for some time. Physician, Psychologist and Author, Dr. Gabriel Maté, has written extensively in relation to the potential lifelong impacts of childhood trauma - manifesting as inflammation, chronic stress, addiction, attention deficit hyperactivity disorder (ADHD), cancer and arthritis, among other debilitating life conditions (Maté, 2022). Throughout his practice and empirical research findings, Dr. Maté emphasises the biopsychosocial nature of humans, and the importance of viewing the mind and body as interconnected when considering any human pathology - as opposed to seeing them as separate entities.

Oprah has made similar observations over the years - elaborated upon in her collaboration with Dr. Bruce Perry, 'What Happened To You'. This offers an in-depth look at what happens to us in our childhood years and how this shapes and defines who we are, how we think, and how we behave and respond to life as adults. Oprah and Dr. Perry give valuable insight and empirical evidence regarding how early trauma can make us behave and react in maladaptive, limiting ways, which if left unchecked, prevents up from reaching our full potential as adults (Winfrey & Perry, 2021).

It takes time, courage and often deep excavation work, to examine the underground emotional roots and branches which inform our unique points of wounding, trauma and nervous system activation. When we come to a place of understanding, as opposed to judgment for how and who we are, we are better able to navigate our internal landscape - taking note of the unsupportive thought patterns which impact our external lives. Cognitive Neuroscientist, Dr. Caroline Leaf discusses this in her wonderful work on brain mapping, where she offers a system of brain awareness and redirection of focus to lead healthier, happier, more enjoyable lives. Leaf proposes that if 'x' is us, and we experience trauma 'y', that doesn't make us 'z' i.e. something different - a label, a disease, a dysfunction, an illness, a problem. Rather, it makes us 'xy' – an integrated version of our former self who experienced a particular life difficulty. (Leaf, 2015, 2021)

Visualisation and Activation Plan for Success

When activating or manifesting life goals, it is helpful to not only dream big, but also to work consciously and consistently toward the attainment of each desired goal - without becoming overly attached to the outcome. Small daily steps, complimented by creative visualisations and feeling into the vibrational energy of that which we most wish to manifest, is what will ultimately amplify our desire and see us through the inevitable bumps and setbacks of life.

Neurosurgeon, Dr. James Doty, in his wonderful work 'Into the Magic Shop', emphasises the importance of engaging the heart as well as mind consciousness when manifesting goals. This ultimately facilitates a broader, kinder intelligence, ensuring we don't become caught up with our own selfish, egotistical gains – rather, that we maintain consciousness for others too. Dr. Doty suggests that goals and desires become infinitely easier to manifest, and even more significantly easier to maintain, if they hold value for the greater good and are not merely for our own selfish pursuit or gain (Doty, 2016).

In other words, if I want to manifest multi billionaire status simply for my own pleasure, that would not be beyond the bounds of limitation (apparently). However, if I intend to use this wealth to help others less fortunate than I - the likelihood of my manifesting and maintaining billionaire status would increase exponentially.

Activate the Green Lights

Being crystal clear about our reasons for wanting to accomplish or manifest goals is what Actor and Author, Mathew McConaughey believes will activate the "green lights" in our lives – the how of where we desire to go. McConaughey's impressive debut book, 'Green Lights', introduces the concept of the 'Egotistical Utilitarian' which identifies the ego as something positive when used in the right way. The ego can drive us forward to achieve many wonderful accomplishments for the greater good - which is both beneficial to us as individuals, as well as to the wider collective (McConaughey, 2020). This inspired me to ponder the potential utilitarian reasons for my meeting Oprah or Graham Norton - Good for me I'm certain, and surely there would be benefits to the wider collective too?! ;) #manifesting

"Who looks outside dreams, who looks inside awakens"
– Carl Jung

Doubt, insecurity and preoccupation with what others think are commonly what stop people from expressing authentically, and assuming the all-important 'Start' position on life's goals and pursuits. Faulty belief systems about how lofty dreams and ambitions may be accessible to others, but not to us, may perpetuate this analysis paralysis, resulting in a continued focus outward whilst ignoring and suppressing the dreams occupied within. Left unattended, this may lead to an unhealthy comparison mind-set with a side-order of low mood, envy or jealousy. Such emotions left unchecked can lead to all kinds of inappropriate projections - including acerbic criticism, gossip, judgment, trolling, and a generally resentful attitude toward anyone or anything living their true purpose, or mirroring that which we may secretly desire.

Negative projections are therefore often unconscious attempts to make us feel better, and whilst this may serve a purpose temporarily, it is extremely short-lived. Feelings of guilt and shame quickly follow as we instinctively know when we're lacking integrity, and violating the laws of human nature. If you know what hurts you, you know what injures others by extension. There may be an initial dopamine hit to receiving that juicy piece of information or gossip - "Did he/she/they really do/say that?", but does it really make anyone feel better to annihilate someone else's character, criticise their actions, judge their appearance, or otherwise? Are we such exemplary humans that we ourselves are positioned to pass judgment? He who casts the first stone etc.....

Newton's Law

There is also Newton's Law to consider - 'For every action there is an equal and opposite reaction'. This essentially means that whatever we choose to put out into the world is in direct proportion to what we will receive in return. Therefore, according to this law - what we say, what we do, how we act and how we treat others, predicts with precision, the energy we will receive in return. Thus, if we're pointing with one finger, we can be sure there are three pointing back. Therefore, when we find ourselves in situations of feeling triggered or wanting to harshly judge, speak badly of or criticise another, we might instead consider pressing the pause button.

By practicing the pause, we often avoid the devastating consequences associated with judgment or criticism - whilst at the same time we allow ourselves time to slow down, breathe and regulate our nervous systems. Once this occurs, we are more suitably composed to get curious about why we may be feeling the need to judge, criticise or put another down. Criticism and judgment are invariably connected to feeling threatened in some way or having a low self-opinion or value. This becomes inappropriately projected onto another in order to feel superficially superior or better.

Triggers and Trauma

"If you spot it, you've got it". Personal triggers and primitive reactions offer us first-hand information about our unique points of wounding, and suggested areas for development. What we react to is essentially where our work lies, yet so often this shadow part of self is that which we most often resist, negate, avoid, suppress or deny. It's easier to point the finger of blame or shame at someone else, rather than examine our own personal achilles' heels or points of wounding. Triggers and negative reactions often reveal secret, unexpressed desires, and thus if we approach our reactions from a place of curiosity, exploration and openness, as opposed to judgment and condemnation - we learn and grow infinitely more.

Swiss Psycholgist, Carl Jung coined the phrase, "Who looks outside dreams, who looks inside, awakens". Awareness of self through practices such as observation, reflection, silence, space, meditation, prayer, mindfulness, movement, therapy and inner child work, foster an enhanced self- awareness as well as compassion - from which everyone benefits, not least of all ourselves. When we are brave enough to acknowledge and explore our triggers and primitive reactions to others, we allow transmutation and transcendence to occur firstly within - which then extends to without.

When we allow the adult, more resourced self to step into the frame, this enables a deep dive into the curious trove of our innermost feelings. Maybe we need of a holiday or break away, and find ourselves reacting to someone who appears to be on permanent vacation? (Note the word 'appears' in each case and remind yourself that things are not always as they seem).Perhaps we're being triggered by someone who has our dream job - whilst we find ourselves out of work, stuck at home, or in a job we dislike? Perhaps we're feeling less than our best physically in our health and appearance, and feeling triggered by someone who we perceive as being happier, healthier, fitter, shapelier, slimmer, stronger? Maybe we're struggling to make ends meet, and find ourselves having a reaction to someone who appears more financially flush?

Action plan for dealing with Triggers

If we find ourselves in a constant state of fight or flight, reacting to everything around us, this means our nervous systems are in an over-activated state, and it is a clear sign that if symptoms persist, we need to seek medical, therapeutic and/or other specialised help.

In addition, the following may be of assistance as functional self-help tools for dealing with negative triggers and reactions:

1) Take time out. Excuse yourself from the triggering situation - if only to go to the bathroom

2) Become aware of and allow your adult, more resourced self to step into the frame

3) Do a body scan and identify where in the body the uncomfortable feeling is being held

4) Welcome and explore the feeling without judgment or condemnation

5) Send breath or energy to the area where the tension is felt

6) Continue breathing - with awareness on slowing your breath to regulate the nervous system

7) Affirm and repeat affirmations such as "I am safe", "All is well", "I am well"

8) Connect and ground yourself with the 5 senses – sight, hearing, taste, touch and smell; naming and taking note of each

9) Continue calming the nervous system with any of the following methods: smelling something you love, drinking something hot and caffeine free, applying a cold compress to the meridian points, getting out into nature, walking barefoot, listening to a beautiful piece of music, journaling, meditation, prayer, yoga, or any other form of silent reflective practice.

10) Using creative visualisation to reframe the situation, circumstance or event.

11) Moving your body to shake the feeling off – literally 'Shake it off' (*cue Taylor Swift)

12) Therapy, inner child and processing work

Dream the dream & Activate the steps to Personal Fulfilment

Whilst many find it easy to commence a task, the follow through is often where most resistance occurs. This explains the many gym memberships as people enter the New Year with great intentions and by January 31st have fallen off the wagon. Invariably, this is because of people not seeing fast enough results or not believing themselves worthy of the time, investment, discipline or consistency required to achieve their desired result. We live in a fast paced world which rewards instant gratification, instant results and immediate success - the best butt without necessarily moving our butt; the best relationship without being a good partner; the best thesis without doing the research; the best title without earning the accolade.

Having fallen off the writing wagon a gazillion times throughout this journey, I can certainly attest to the procrastination/perfectionist loop! - wanting the impressive result, and simultaneously doubting and stalling my practice. Or making a decent start, but editing and re-editing to the point of a critical blank page staring back. In the early stages of my writing journey, I used just about every excuse in the book (no pun intended) to avoid or delay the task in hand. Finally, I got tired of my own B.S. and decided if I wanted a completed work, I needed to take consistent, affirmative action - paying less attention to fearful thoughts and the notion of a perfect final submission!

The interesting point with procrastination is that whilst we think we're gaining satisfaction from task avoidance or delay, in reality the avoidance merely heightens feelings of anxiety. This brings forth a diminished sense of self-worth and a loss in confidence, due to not committing or following through on our deepest intentions and desires.

Whilst our inherent worthiness is never compromised by what we do or don't accomplish in life, somehow when something feels connected to our life's mission and purpose, we hold an acute sense of time - our most valuable commodity, being irrevocably swindled. This leads to further feelings of guilt, anxiety and restlessness, for which the only antidote, is to take immediate resourceful action.

"To begin, begin."
– William Wordsworth

Start, however small, in whatever capacity, and build from there. On any given day, we may fall short of our best intentions - we get distracted; we get pulled away; we fall off the wagon, COVID-19 strikes; a family member becomes ill; a hot date presents. Rather than complaining, be-rating ourselves, lamenting over time being lost or a situation not being perfectly played out as we had imagined - a better option is to gently acknowledge where we're at, re-commit to the process, visualise the end goal, and simply keep on keepin' on!

Although I had many writing sabbaticals, my mission or 'why' for completing this work was evidently larger than any of my best excuses. Deep down, I believed I had something worthwhile to say, which I hoped would be of benefit to others too, and although I experienced several episodes of fear, self–doubt, procrastination and perfectionism - I carried on regardless!

Small steps win the race

Results take time, accomplishments take time, so instead of thinking about the quickest, shortest route to success - in the words of Cheryl Sandberg, "lean into" the pathway to success, or "play the long game" as recommended by Social Media Mogul, Gary Vee. This simply requires us to show up consciously and consistently, committing to spend time - whether five minutes or five hours working on our desired project or goal. Bear in mind this doesn't have to involve the big stuff, it can apply to literally any area of our lives where we wish to make an improvement or change.

For example, maybe it's taking a fifteen minute walk in the fresh air at lunchtime instead of sitting indoors for the entire break; maybe it's reading or listening to an informative book or podcast instead of "Netflix and chill"; maybe it's zipping our mouths and checking ourselves before gossiping, criticising or making a judgment on another; maybe it's going to the gym instead of sleeping late. Positive, progressive options are endless. However, we invariably have to dig deep and "stack our habits" in order to lock them in as 'automatic daily processes' - as suggested in James Clear's bestseller, 'Atomic Habits'.

#DrDee

How we do something is how we do everything

The interesting point with making a single positive change to one area in our lives, is that it very often reverberates to other areas too - evoking an impressive domino effect. How we do one thing essentially becomes how we do everything - and by taking small, consistent daily steps to stretch and improve ourselves, we cement affirmative habits that then become entire operating systems. Whilst the cumulative effects of investing daily time and energy into our mental, emotional, physical, psychological, spiritual and social health, doesn't preclude or guarantee immunity from life's inevitable struggles, it does provide a positive framework for dealing with and responding to whatever challenges emerge.

We also become more empowered and self-assured in the process. Thus, taking regular disciplined action and locking in good habits along the way - not only predisposes us to making valued progress, but neuroplasticity studies have shown that our brains adapt in both structure and function to accommodate newly positive ways of thinking and behaving. "The brain literally takes the shape of what our minds and bodies most often rest upon."(Rick Hanson)

Applying Structure and Routine to Achieve Small Daily Wins

As part of my personal development journey, I have a morning ritual which I have practiced, edited and revised over the years. Each morning first thing, I use intention setting, creative visualisation, gratitude, prayer and affirmations to set the tone for my day. This serves to assist in maintaining a mindful focus, and whilst some days I'm without doubt more poised than others, it's a practice I wouldn't be without. I believe having a morning ritual enables me to be of greatest value and support to those with whom I connect with daily, and whilst an adjustment or several may be required on any one day!, the practice sets me up with the tools to remain focused on the important stuff. If at any moment I find myself becoming derailed or negatively triggered, I am more readily aware of the necessary recalibration steps I need to take to return to a space of calm.

Morning rituals and routines come highly recommended by some of the most luminary thought leaders throughout the world - many of whom have inspired my brightest moments and influenced part-content of this book. These include, (in no particular order): Martin Seligman, William James, Carl Jung, Joseph Campbell, Oprah Winfrey, Deepak Chopra, Don Miguel Ruiz, Paulo Coelho, Marianne Williamson, Gabrielle Bernstein, Russell Brand, Lewis Howes, James Doty, Gabor Mate, Shefali Tsabary, Eckhart Tolle, Wayne Dyer, Neville Goddard, Jay Shetty, Tony Robbins, Robin Sharma, Gary Zukav, Caroline Leaf, Brene Brown, Elizabeth Gilbert, Susan Cain, Nicole LePera, Danielle La Porte, Sarah Ban Breathnach, Dale Carnegie, Kim Dolan Leto, Joel Osteen, Kimberly Jones, Esther Perel, Emily Morse, Daniel Amen, Rick Hanson to name a few.

Amongst their inspired teachings, most if not all of these leaders advocate some form of sacrosanct morning regimen, which sets the tone for the remainder of the day. By consciously and consistently calibrating the mind, body and spirit to their highest possible frequency, we prime our capacity to assist in practicing optimism, expansive thought, instinctive right action, reduced reactivity, and enhanced relationships with others.

Physical Wellbeing and Health

Studies have offered robust evidence, that actively moving our bodies and working up a sweat is also a potential buffer to stress and managing our mental health (Lehrer & Woolfolk, 2021). The discipline of exercise, regardless of how motivated we '"feel" or what the mind may tell us, is another obvious success marker toward maintaining physical and psychological health. The trick is to find what works for you, and stick to it!

For example, I know I'm not the best at exercising first thing in the morning - particularly during cold, Irish winters, so there's an infinitely better chance of me locking in exercise as an evening activity. To this end, I generally run in the evenings and although I don't always feel like running, experience has taught me that I always feel better afterward. I have therefore trained my mind to make this a non-negotiable contract with self, which reinforces a sense of confidence and self-reliance. The mind will offer a million ways to distract, deter and take us off course from our goals, however daily discipline and positive habit stacking re-inforce positive daily and ultimate life-long habits.

Exercise is another way of healing and strengthening the mind and physical body, since we're practicing situations of getting past what's mentally and physically uncomfortable, whilst simultaneously building resilience (LePera, 2021). Another way of doing this is through cold showers as per Iceman, Wim Hof's recommendation. Admittedly, I haven't really perfected the art of this myself - much as I admire those who plunge into the icy Atlantic first thing in the morning! However, I understand the psychology around exposing ourselves to the uncomfortable - which leads to self-confirmation that we can indeed accomplish and overcome whatever the mind often desperately resists or fears. In cases where severe anxiety is present, exposure to feared stimuli may need to be guided by a professional Psychologist, and take place in a systemised fashion - known as systematic desensitisation, from least feared stimulus to most feared.

Short to Medium Term Goals

A per my Wellness Recovery Action Planning (WRAP) research described earlier in Chapter 1, in addition to using daily self-management tools as a way of maintaining positive mental health, WRAP can also be useful in establishing weekly, monthly and long term goals - without becoming overly attached to timelines or outcomes. If COVID-19 taught us anything, it's that we need to remain flexible and fluid with our plans, timelines, agendas and attitudes! Having a roadmap of sorts helps to keep us on track as well as enabling us to remain accountable, and since what we give our attention to largely impacts who and what we become, this is a worthy consideration within the context of creating successful long term habits.

Short to medium term goals can be anything from work related, to fitness and dietary related - or any other area of our lives we feel deserves attention. It helps when we have a framework or intended trajectory, whilst still being mindful of the sanctity of each moment and how quickly things can change. Invariably and inevitably, we are likely to get derailed or interrupted at certain points on our journey and life path, and although our instinct may be to kick, scream and curse the tidal flow, a more adaptive response is to lean into the current as best we can, reminding ourselves that nothing is forever.

> **"In order to receive the best from the world,**
> **we must give our best to the world"**
> **- Oprah**

Success is self-defined. We get to decide what constitutes our personal definition of success. In Maslow's Hierarchy of Needs (Maslow, 1943), human development begins and must be fulfilled at foundation level first, before evolving higher - to the highest point of self-actualisation. In other words, we must master the basic fundamentals first, before we can aspire and evolve to greater heights. There are a number of factors which play an important role toward achieving the small daily wins - which I believe are what cumulatively translate to the ultimate success markers, and for me include:

1) How consistent I've been in my morning ritual
2) How much I've slept the night before
3) How much I've exercised
4) What I have/haven't eaten
5) How is my thought behaviour – am I allowing negative thoughts, ruminations or resentments to accumulate and get stuck, or am I in a space of awareness and letting go?
6) Am I making time for creative visualisation, meditation, affirmations and prayer?
7) Am I stimulated cognitively - taking daily steps to learn and evolve my thinking through books, podcasts, conversations, reading and listening?
8) Am I connected with like-minded people, with whom I feel supported and celebrated or are the flames to my fire being quashed by others' jealousy or unconscious negative projections?

#DrDee

9) Am I expressing myself creatively – via writing, journaling, making time for music, fashion, travel, art, conversation, connection, intimacy?

10) Am I connected socially? Do I need to call or connect with a friend or mentor?

11) Am I communicating freely, creatively and authentically, or am I suppressing, people pleasing and censoring?

12) If I notice I'm being triggered by someone, what adjustment do I need to make internally, as opposed to making a judgment on the other?

13) Am I trying to over-control things, or am I in a place of doing what I can in each life aspect, whilst trusting in divine timing?

14) Am I showing up with my best on any given day in each life area?

15) Am I regularly reviewing, editing, changing and updating various aspects of my life?

16) Am I living my true purpose?

17) Am I working consistently toward the attainment of my goals?

18) Am I using my God-given talents, gifts and abilities?

19) Am I offering my time, sharing my gifts, and being of service to others?

"The two most important days of our lives are the day we were born and the day we find out why."
– Mark Twain

EXERCISE, BODY IMAGE
AND LIFE TRAJECTORIES

Exercise in Context

Many of us are aware of the benefits of exercise as it relates to physical health, though somewhat less familiar with the impact of exercise on mental health. Exercise is something which is regularly recommended by medical professionals to improve illnesses - such as cardiovascular disease, obesity and diabetes, however it remains largely under-prescribed in stabilising mental health (Windeman et al. 2020). As someone who has exercised pretty much all of my life, I firmly believe in the powerful potency of exercise. It is something to which I passionately extol the benefits of to my clients, as a highly effective tool for relieving stress, improving confidence, focusing the mind, and elevating the spirit.

Physiological & Psychological Benefits

From a basic scientific perspective, exercise releases happy hormones in the brain, known as endorphins. Endorphins are the body's natural pain-killers and are associated with positive mood, life force and wellbeing - so when we exercise, we're essentially stimulating the natural feel good factor of the body, both physically and chemically. Serotonin, referred to as the happy chemical, is a neurotransmitter which is targeted largely by antidepressant medication. Serotonin is triggered and increased when we exercise, which creates knock-on positive side effects, such as improvements to mood and self-confidence. Many studies have effectively demonstrated the benefits of exercise in reducing anger, improving mood states, reducing anxiety and improving measures of depression (Russo et al, 2020). This is not to suggest that exercise should be substituted for medication where this is required – however, it's worth considering the benefits of exercise as an additional support tool to maintaining positive mental health and physical wellbeing.

My Journey

Exercise has featured in some shape or form throughout my life. After graduating from University College Dublin (UCD) with a Degree in Psychology and Postgraduate Diploma in Business Studies (UCD Smurfit School), I set about attending to some bucket list activities. Travel and gaining a Fitness Instructor's qualification ranked high on my list, so to kick things off, travel was awarded priority. I had been dating a guy from the Netherlands during my postgraduate year, so that seemed like a pretty good place to start. Despite a few initial teething problems - including my bags being lost on in transit, and being without clothes for the first week (the absolute trauma of it all!) I had a total blast and ended up staying there for over three weeks.

During that time, I was introduced to the sights, sounds, people, "coffee shops" and culture of Holland - which was a trip to say the least! I returned home, completely buzzing from the experience and itching to go travelling again – this time to South East Asia and Australia. I had just begun planning my trip, when out of the blue I received a call from a college pal. He too was bitten by the wanderlust bug, and happened to hear I had similar travel ideas. After a two-hour phone-call, we had successfully mapped our trip, to include a couple of nights in Bangkok, then on to Koh Samui, next on to Bali, before finally arriving in Sydney,

Australia. *Will refer more to the year spent in Australia later in this chapter, but suffice it to say at this point, it was an amazing experience, and hugely significant for me personally.

Fitness Instructor Qualification

After fourteen epic months of living, working, traveling and road trippin', I returned home to the land of the living, and set about completing a Fitness Instructor's training qualification. Lured by the glamour and feel-good factor I experienced whilst attending fitness classes at UCD, and having become an avid gym in Australia, it seemed like a natural progression. I began my Fitness Instructor Training course, and six months later, received my professional qualification. Almost immediately, I began teaching in the Fitness Industry part-time, which served as a useful, rewarding, and hugely enjoyable side-line for many years to follow. I taught in various clubs, gyms and university sports centres - and aside from the seemingly constant battle through peak traffic to make a 6pm class-setup, I loved the buzz of teaching and being part of a large, energetic group. Far from feeling like work - for me, it was an amazing opportunity to stay fit, whilst being paid for the privilege.

High Kicks and Clinical Trials

Alongside teaching fitness classes, I held steadfast to my vision of becoming a Clinical Psychologist, and had begun working to build up my portfolio of clinical training experience. As anyone who has walked a similar path can attest, the clinical application process is tough and hugely competitive - demanding resilience, tenacity, and brass lady-balls! Dealing with the all-too frequent knockbacks, setbacks, disappointments and rejections - which are pretty much par for course, isn't easy. However, I was relentless and determined to achieve what I believed would bring me professional fulfilment. During the early noughties, I undertook a Masters in Psychology at the University of Ulster, Belfast, before working in various hospitals, residential care settings, and nursing home facilities, to build up my portfolio of clinical experience.

My CV was sent to just about every Psychologist in the country - accompanied by a "Please give me a job as an Assistant Psychologist" cover letter. I'm paraphrasing obviously, but receiving little if any response from the majority - apart from the occasional P.F.O., the ability to stay optimistic and hopeful was certainly a challenge. Assistant Psychology posts weren't very plentiful in Ireland - and still aren't to this day, and of those occasionally advertised, every aspiring Psychologist in the country is on the case.

A Chink of Light

On a sunny June Bank Holiday weekend, amidst the application hustle, my Mum ventured to Galway for girl-chats and to use the vouchers she had received from family the previous Christmas. In keeping with annual tradition, we went to a well-known department store, and in a classically Irish Mammy way, my mother struck up a conversation with the lady assisting. This lady's son happened to be a Clinical Psychologist who worked locally, and on hearing my situation, she gave me his number, advising I give him a call - and to tell him that she sent me!

By this time I was triple-jobbing - working as a part time Healthcare Assistant, part-time Fitness Instructor and an HSE administrator. I had this Clinical Psychologist guy's number on speed-dial, and continued to hound him with only slightly creepy, "I met your Mum in a Department store" phone messages! One day, evidently realising, this girl is never going away - he took my call. We chatted briefly, arranged a meeting, and as the saying goes - the rest is history. I began working under his supervision as a Voluntary Assistant Psychologist – yep, no mon, hon, but at that point it was a case of, "Exploit me? Why, sure!" This for me, was another robust stepping stone, to securing one of the coveted clinical training places, and I was thrilled to receive any opportunity to work under formal supervision.

To support myself financially, I continued working in the HSE during the day, whilst teaching fitness classes in the evenings, and I will remain forever grateful to my then boss at University College Hospital,

Galway - now sadly deceased, who facilitated many hours of my early Psychology career development. He allowed me to work flexible hours, and took a genuine interest in my academic and career progression from the outset - always urging me forward. Meanwhile in the evenings, my fitness classes were booming! Everything from TaeBo to Spinning, Pilates, Body Attack, Body Conditioning and Boxercise were among my Instructor mix - all of which required continuous professional updating to remain on the cutting edge of safe, effective and progressive practice.

Power in Purpose

Teaching Fitness classes offered an amazing insight into the power of exercise to music, as well as the power of the group – to support, uplift and to help transcend people's mood, energy and spirit. It was active mindfulness at its finest - before people even knew or understood the term! Participants could literally lose themselves for an hour, and reap the positive rewards and benefits afterward. The experience offered a wonderful insight into what I now know to be my life's purpose – to lift, inspire, encourage, lead and support people to recognise, and reach for their brightest and best.

Rejection, Tenacity, Feedback & Knowing Who You Are

As time progressed, the will to stay on the Clinical Training Application route was becoming less attractive. Rejection reportedly lights up the same area of the brain as the pain of a broken limb (Weir, 2012). That feeling of being so close to the finish line, yet somehow not being chosen for the final cut is something to which we can all relate, and unless we have the appropriate coping tools for building ourselves back up, we can internalise the rejection and perceive it as something personal. I had become utterly consumed with the clinical application process – to the point of my entire self-worth appearing to hinge solely on whether or not I was in the final shake-up for a training place.

As professionally advised, I dialled myself up research and experience wise, and dimmed myself down style wise. The advice that was given to me by a Senior Clinical Psychologist was, "Tie your hair back in a bun for the interviews Denise (pre top knots being in any way cool!), and wear a dark coloured suit." Really? So you mean my John Travolta-esque Saturday Night Fever white trouser suit is out of the question then?! Despite efforts to accordingly comply, contorting myself into something which felt increasingly unnatural - suffice it to say, I was becoming increasingly disillusioned by the selection process.

Around about this time, a previously forwarded CV for a temporary Acting Psychology post with a large Irish organisation, led to my being called for interview. Without any major thought or expectation, I gave it my best shot – the up-shot of which was my being successfully appointed. To this day, I thank my lucky stars that there was once again another wonderful gentleman - then Principal Psychologist, on the interview panel. He later said he saw my potential from the outset, and continued to champion, support and encourage me, until his sad, untimely death.

We need people like that in our lives (and I've been blessed with many!) The special souls who cross our paths at seemingly just the right moment, who encourage and believe in our potential - when we least have belief in ourselves.

Experience and Insight

As I became familiar with my work, I also became more certain of what truly set my soul on fire. I was fortunate to have been exposed to pretty much all types of Clinical presentations in my new role - with the exception of very young children, and throughout this process I realised my areas of specialist interest included Adult Mental Health and Acquired Brain Injury (hence my Doctoral research subject areas).

As Psychologists, our primary goal is the alleviation of human suffering and distress, and to this end, our work centres primarily around assessment, treatment, intervention and research. I understood from early on,

#DrDee

that the fundamental basis for assisting people most effectively, lay in equipping them with the appropriate skills, tools and strategies, to better support a healthy internal framework, whilst signposting people also to the appropriate external, community supports. I was immensely happy in the work I was doing, and was super excited to be learning so much - with literal text book presentations coming to life in reality each day. Around about then, I made the informed decision, I no longer wished to further pursue the Clinical application process.

My investment - which had previously felt all-consuming, had waned, and remarkably, it no longer held the same point of power in my consciousness. I was confident that I would find another way to complete my professional and academic studies in Psychology to the highest possible standard. This resulted in my pulling the one and only clinical application I had submitted for that year - just prior to the first round of interviews. It would have been my fourth round of immersion in the process had I chosen to proceed with interview, and whilst this may be a shock to some - for anyone reading this who has walked, or is walking a similar path, this is neither a unique nor remarkable story. Although some strike gold in their earlier application attempts, many are left similarly consumed and bewildered by the long, arduous, and seemingly elusive process.

More than one way to skin a cat!

For me, it was time to move on. I had reached a point where I was no longer in a place of obsessional attachment to the traditional clinical training and progression route in Ireland, and decided instead to explore alternative progression pathways overseas. By this time, I had developed a heightened awareness of various creative interests I additionally wished to pursue, and whilst I held an overall vision of where my career and professional aspirations lay, I was less rigidly attached to the idea of an exact final destination or outcome.

I began my Practitioner Doctorate in City University, London, in 2012 whilst continuing to work full time - let's just say I had no life for those three and a half years….in fact, I was a complete nerd! Once again, I was very fortunate to have unrivalled support and supervision. One of my Doctoral Supervisors, was a gentleman who was Head of my Psychology Masters programme in Belfast, and although he was retired and no doubt, had infinitely better things to do than supervise my studies, he very graciously agreed. Each month, he travelled from Belfast to Dublin to provide formal clinical supervision, and to this day I credit the timely completion of my Doctoral studies to his consistency, guidance, academic excellence, professionalism, kindness and relentless support. I was also fortunate to have the guidance and support of my academic supervisor based in City University, London, who additionally provided telephonic, email, and in-person support as required.

As I alluded to earlier - we are only ever as good as the people with whom we surround ourselves, and this is especially the case when selecting pro-fessional and academic supervisors, as well as work and lifestyle mentors.

I completed my Doctorate in 2015, achieving one of my most aspired to academic goals. The moral of the story? Where there's a will there's a way – and often, with many alternative routes! Trust the trajectory of your life and follow your gut. Nature has a way of guiding us to where we're supposed to be - so do your best, embrace the journey, remain open and flexible, and change the script whenever you feel inspired to do so. Good things come to those who remain patient, grateful, flexible - and work their asses off in the process!

Run your own race

Due to the time restraints of working full-time, and undertaking my Doctorate, I reluctantly made the decision to finish up teaching fitness classes. I took up running instead, which was something I had previously done - and continue to this day. Hitting the road for me, is as much a sanity project, as it is vanity, and a regular 7/8k feels fresh and liberating. It clears my head, heightens my senses, and invigorates my spirit - and whilst there are obvious benefits to being in good physical shape, nothing surpasses feeling good mentally and emotionally.

To date I've ran one marathon - New York, which as marathons go, I probably couldn't have picked better! Departing from Galway with a great crew, in aid of a wonderful charity, we had a brief and amazing weekend. The marathon was super atmospheric - littered with cheering, enthusiastic fans, and although it was one of the biggest mental endurance tests I've ever experienced - it will most likely remain the first and last of its kind! I found the preparation beastly, and was never as sick or as run-down as when I was clocking up those 26 training miles. On the upside, I experienced first-hand, the incredible power of the mind in carrying us beyond the wall of extreme physical pain and exhaustion - not to mention the obvious benefits of being surrounded by positive, uplifting energy from start to finish. You have to hand it to the Americans - they certainly know how to cheer people on!

Stride with Pride

These days, deciding my own mileage feels more in-synch with my body's natural rhythm, and whilst certain times/days it's a struggle to get out (particularly on cold winter's evenings), I've found that on those exact evenings when I least feel like running, I most need to run! When I'm on the road, I remind myself of what a privilege it is to have the use of my limbs, and think of the people - some very close to my heart, who are compromised in their health and mobility and would literally give their eye-teeth to independently go for a walk or run. In so doing, any feelings of discomfort or disgruntlement are quickly replaced with feelings of gratitude, motivation and inspiration to keep challenging myself and moving the needle forward.

As my foot-strike hits the road, I use this non-negotiable training time, to observe the sights, sounds, tastes, smells and sensations - which enables me (mostly!) to enter a mindful, energised state. However, on some occasions, it's a case of, "Just get the job done!" There will always be things in life that we know are good for us, but don't necessarily enjoy doing all the time - and that's when discipline kicks in. Do it, even when you don't "feel" like doing it, and through the process, the mind becomes strengthened, the habit becomes reinforced and our confidence begins to soar.

Ponder to Propel

In 2012, I travelled to Addis Ababa, Ethiopia, with another amazing crew. We completed a 10K charity race, which was organised and led by a literal Earth-Angel – who went out of his way to make the trip fun and memorable for everyone. One of my abiding recollections of the race, was firstly the speed at which the Ethiopians ran! Many, in little light canvas training pumps, which were the furthest thing from shock proof you can imagine! Yet they ran with beaming smiles and happy hearts - stopping to dance, have fun and enjoy the music along the way. It was pure joy, embodied and exemplified in its simplest, most contagious form. We were also very lucky to experience many other cultural and memorable moments in Ethiopia - one of which was a trip to the orphanages.

Apart from the stark conditions - the sad, forlorn look on the little babies' faces is something I'll never forget. They lay in their cots silently, never crying - because sadly, they knew that no-one was there to pick them up. This experience and others, are among those I call upon, if feeling demotivated, victimised or in any way sorry for myself! They quickly change my state to a place of gratitude for the luxury of having first-world problems, the privilege of clean running water, the use of my legs, and the ability to run in shock absorbent runners! There are always moments worth readily calling to mind, when we need to occupy a more grateful, elevated state.

Activate to Motivate

The notion of activation preceding motivation is a concept to which I very often refer when working with clients who are feeling demotivated or struggling with finding their mojo. As humans, we often make the mistake of believing that in order to become activated, we must first become motivated - when the reverse is often the case. When we begin

#DrDee

something new, it may feel initially challenging and tough, however if we persist - refusing to give into our limiting thoughts, beliefs and default behaviour patterns, we eventually build strength and momentum. For example, if we begin a gym exercise programme, it may initially feel difficult, but over time, with persistence and discipline, it gets easier - perhaps even enjoyable! Anything worthwhile takes time - requiring us to dig deep, remain consistent, and keep our eyes on the prize!

Exercise and Body Dysmorphia

As I alluded to earlier, exercise has pretty much always featured in my life to date - mainly for health and enjoyment reasons. At certain times in the past however, it featured for very different reasons. As someone who suffered with body dysmorphia and an eating diorder - on and off from the age of sixteen to thirty-one, exercise played a significant role in both the maintenance of the dysfunction, and in my recovery also.

The disordered eating became initially activated over a summer period, when a friend and I went to work in a hotel away from home on our school summer holidays. I had just turned sixteen and had begun dating a guy who had just returned from holidays for the summer season - looking tanned and hawwwt! I was working typical bar hours, and eating at irregular times - when randomly, one day I came across a magazine article which told the story of a girl who used an eating disorder as a way of controlling her weight. The article immediately caught my attention as despite being slim (for reference, I was a UK size 10; US size 4/6 at the time) I nevertheless, had a palpable fear of putting on weight.

I was someone who was raised in a very high achieving family – the youngest of six children, there was considerable emphasis placed on education and achievement. Appearance, weight and attractiveness were also heavily weighted, and I have clear recollections of my father going on week-long crazy restriction diets, running in rubber suits, grinding it out for hours on a stationary bicycle, and sweating away the excess in an old style sauna in our family home. My mother was similarly weight conscious - though much less torturously so! She attended weekly keep fit classes, often referring to how she couldn't afford to put on weight due to her petite frame.

Looking back at the few childhood photographs that exist, I was somewhat podgy – but to no remarkable extent. I recall receiving a lot of attention for how I looked from an early age, to which my mother would modestly deflect with, "Don't be giving her notions" - a classic Irish Mammy response, in case you'd become "too full of yourself". One of my brothers also used to jokingly sing the melody of the popular Coke add, "Coke is it", replacing the words with "Neesie's fat". He was being funny and in no way ill-intended, however somehow the message unconsciously penetrated, and this, combined with the aforementioned backdrop, left me with some pretty warped ideas about appearance, size, body image, and what was or wasn't acceptable.

Without deliberate intent or malice on anyone's part, you might say my programming was a little off from the start, which of course wasn't helped by my having an already sensitive personality predisposition. At the age of fifteen, any self-consciousness already present, became further exacerbated when I went out with a guy who had a similar preoccupation with appearance and weight. He considered it comedy gold to comment on how people looked, and unfortunately stumbled upon the realisation that weight struck a sensitive chord for me. Once again, without knowledge or understanding of the damaging effects, he would laugh and joke that he wouldn't be going out with me if he actually believed I was "fat" – "Because I knew I wasn't, right?"

Body Talks

Had my sense of self-worth been more robust and built upon sturdier things than physical appearance, weight and size - neither comments, jokes, magazine articles, pictures or otherwise would have held any real or lasting impact on how I viewed myself. Implicitly, I would have known that we are so much more than our physical size and body measurements. As time progressed, the need to weigh myself several times per day or to look at my body's reflection in shameful disgust would have been a non-issue, and I would have respected and valued my body for the amazing powerhouse I now know, and appreciate it to be.

Our bodies work tirelessly every day, to support, function and carry us through life. They are not mere aesthetic features - to be internally shamed, rejected, abused and bullied into a certain size or standard of conformity. They deserve upmost respect and the very best of nourishment for all the work they do to support and accommodate us each day. Sadly, body dysmorphia and eating disorders are complex in nature, and play dangerous tricks with the mind, body, heart and soul - resulting in shallow, disordered thinking, among other negative complications.

Acknowledging the Problem

It was my second year in university, before I fully acknowledged that the relationship I had with my body and food, was distorted. Things had progressed to a more serious level and I decided to seek an appointment with the Psychologist on campus. Until that point, I had been convincing myself that what I had wasn't that serious and that I could stop at any moment. The problem was I couldn't. Despite repeated attempts to make positive changes - by the time I sought therapeutic support, I was in the early part of my second year in university, living on campus, and intermittently bingeing, purging, starving as well as obsessively running around the dark, icy campus fields at the crack of dawn. I managed to somehow maintain an external polished image with clothes, makeup and accessories - which of course was completely at odds with how I was feeling on the inside. I felt guilty, fat, out of control, disgusting, hopeless, gross, and worst of all - I was too embarrassed and ashamed to tell anyone.

Burned by two previous confessional attempts - the gossip laden repercussions of which did little to inspire me to share my struggle ever again, certain protective factors remained thankfully intact. These included that I always had great friends, was popular, and ironically - socially extrovert. Although I felt trapped and constrained on the inside - outwardly I managed to lead a pretty normal life, with college lectures, nights out and friends - many of whom remain wonderful pals to this day. I also had periods of symptom reprieve, where I managed to white-knuckle it and keep things under control, before eventually pressing that all too familiar self-destruct button once again.

Seeking Help & Support

The Psychologist I attended on campus, was a very glamorous, professional lady. She was personable and easy to chat to - not too serious, and made reference to the fact that she herself had suffered an eating disorder in her earlier years, from which she had successfully recovered. It's interesting because as practicing Clinicians, we're taught to be very boundaried with our vulnerabilities and personal lives, and yet this exact admission from a professional, was what established instant connection and rapport - allowing me to feel immediately understood and at ease.

The Psychologist could evidently relate on both a personal and professional level with the shame and embarrassment I felt, and how difficult I found it to open up. She reassured me I was going to be fine, adding that she believed I fell into the profile of individuals who develop eating disorders and body dysmorphia, as a result of being disproportionately influenced by popular fashion culture, magazines and TV shows. She was curious however, as to why I was reluctant to tell my parents and family. I relayed my fear that they wouldn't understand and I was worried about being negatively perceived, judged or criticised. I believed they would expect more of me - as though I should somehow be beyond such triviality. She agreed that if I felt making a disclosure would exacerbate matters, my reservations were warranted.

Ironically, my assessment of matters was somewhat confirmed on a random weekend home soon afterward. My sister and I had just done the weekend shop with our Mum, and whilst we sat outside in the car, my sister turned to me and said, "You'd want to cop on". Clearly she had a sense of what was going on - however unfortunately, had as little knowledge or understanding of the complexity of the issue as I or anyone else. I couldn't explain, nor did I have sufficient insight or understanding myself to articulate what felt like something that was beyond my choosing or control. I was suffering and needed help, but didn't know who or where to extend my net. In that moment of high emotional intensity, it was clear that both my sister and I were of a similar mind-set – I needed to cop on, and fast!

I resolved to do better, be better, try harder. But it seemed the more I tried, the more obsessed and ashamed I became. My symptoms were an everyday preoccupation - body weight, image, size, eating, not eating, weighing food, not weighing food, bingeing, purging, restricting, starving, exercise, more exercise, no exercise, mirrors, no mirrors, how fat I was, how thin I was, how much weight I lost, how much weight I gained, how much others must be thinking about my weight and how fat I was, where/when/how I was going to control my next meal, where/when/how I was going to get rid of it....

Complete and utter C-R-A-Z-Y T-O-W-N!!

Protective Factors

Once again, despite the insanity of it all, there were a few important protective factors which remained intact. As Psychologists we always look to establish protective factors when people are struggling with complex issues. They may be anything from a significant person/s, activities, hobbies or other coping mechanisms, which offer temporary relief from the presenting problem. Protectors enable people to somehow function within their dysfunction, and in many cases facilitate temporary reprieve.

In my case - for certain days, weeks and discreet periods of time, I managed to experience freedom and symptom relief - and during these times, I would feel great, hopeful that I had finally cracked the monster on my back - before inevitably self sabotaging once again. Feeling powerless, pathetic and out of control, my self talk was anything but kind and compassionate. What the hell was wrong with me? Why couldn't I just get things under control? Why couldn't I just get it together like everyone else?

Due to a large waiting list and I suspect being under-resourced, I had just four sessions with the Psychologist on campus. My appointments were monthly, and she recognised a pattern - my most vulnerable time appeared to be on the weekends, when I went home to my parents. Upon my return to campus, I would spend the week punishing myself with extreme behaviours and self-loathing, attempting to compensate for whatever perceived damage I believed I had done at the weekend. Once again, the Psychologist recommended I confide in my parents and family for support – however, the shame and embarrassment was simply too much. Once again, I remained tight-lipped.

Around that time, I came across a twelve-step programme for people with disordered eating which I began attending. Although I was the youngest in the group by a country mile, I met some of the kindest, most genuine people, which slowly enabled me to find my authentic voice. This alleviated some of the burden I was shamefully carrying, and allowed me to connect with others who walked a similar path. Each week I showed up and applied the steps to the best of my ability, and although the often doom and gloom atmosphere didn't quite jam for me at the meetings - I continued attending and was immensely grateful for the shared connections and support.

One weekend whilst home and sitting by the fire watching TV with my Dad, I spontaneously opened up. Although visibly shocked, he reacted calmly and was keen to know how the problem could be fixed. Daddy urged me to get whatever help and support I needed, and offered to pay for private therapy sessions for as long as was required. I asked if he could keep it to himself until such time as I felt stronger and more comfortable telling others, to which he agreed. However, I suspect worry got the better of him, and he further discussed with my Mum.

My 'secret' was finally out, and dealt with in a manner similar to most emotionally repressed Irish families - never spoken about (at least not to me). I suspect no-one really knew how best to deal with the issue, having never previously been exposed to anything similar. My Mum immediately went into worry mode - impressing upon me how thin she believed I was. Once again, neither she nor I, nor anyone else fully realising - that weight, physical appearance, food and body related struggles are merely the tip of the iceberg – physical manifestations of a much deeper emotional struggle.

During this time, my parents had been having difficulties in their marriage which resulted in verbal arguments and general tension in our family home. Of course this was something I had neglected to tell the Psychologist I was attending at UCD, which I suspect would have altered her assessment and formulation of matters. I had grown accustomed to keeping the window dressed - presenting things in the most palatable manner and putting on a brave front, fearing perhaps if I spoke words of malaise or discord - that would somehow make them true.

My parents ultimately separated, and my attempt to deal with this was to block it out - denying the obvious potential that this might ever happen. I did this by escaping to my room, blasting music in my ears, and gorging myself on high carb, sugary and fatty foods. This temporary induced food coma, was for a moment my escape, my refuge, my protector, my drug. Like any addiction, it enabled me to not have to temporarily think, feel or deal with life in an adult manner - I could simply zone out and numb my feelings, whilst ignoring everything else that was happening around me.

As with any and all addictions, this temporary oblivion was quickly followed by intense feelings of self-disgust, guilt, shame, repulsion, rejection, self-hatred and a monologue of self-abuse. The desire to purge and punish myself in the worst way possible became my next heightened obsession – once again, a disordered attempt at gaining control over a situation, when everything around me appeared to be out of my control.

Light in the Darkness

I referred earlier to my trip to Australia, where I had an amazing year of travel and self-discovery. I was at this time, in my early 20's and my parents were separating. Maybe I was running away, maybe I was searching for answers, maybe I needed time-out. Whatever the case, I felt liberated by the wonder and novelty of being far away, with so many new and accessible adventures and experiences. These included surfing, climbing, white water rafting, swimming with the sharks, bungee jumping, body boarding, opera, outdoor concerts, Christmas on the beach, traveling up the East coast and so much more I got to live and experience.

I met up with an Irish guy who to this day I credit as being instrumental to my recovery. He crossed my path within the first couple of weeks of my arrival in Sydney - once again consolidating my belief that the right people show up at just the right moment. We weren't going out for very long, when I spotted an advertisement for a weekend retreat in The Blue Mountains for people with food and body related issues. Feeling too embarrassed to say where I was going, I simply asked that he trust I was going somewhere I needed to be, and that's exactly what he did – no questions, no judgment, no jealousy. His response inspired my confidence in him as a pretty cool camper, and upon my return, I relayed the whole story. This was the first time I had allowed a guy into my heavily guarded secret - and to my surprise, he wasn't even remotely phased or bothered. He simply listened with kindness and empathy, and from there, supported me with whatever I needed to work on with my recovery.

Paulo Coelho in his compelling book, 'The Alchemist' proposes that in order for us to achieve what he refers to as our "personal legend", different people are sent to us in our journeys throughout life. I am in no doubt that this guy was one of those serendipitous encounters, and I will remain forever grateful to him - and the many other divine encounters and connections I have experienced in various guises along the way. Through the love and support I received, I found my way back from chaos and destruction, to health, happiness, freedom and recovery.

While in Australia, my recovery was easily maintained through consistent practice and routine. This included daily reflections, weekly attendance at positive support group meetings, exercise, healthy diet, monthly appointments with a specialised dietician, sunshine, blue skies, and unrivalled personal support. Shortly after arriving home however, familiar triggers resurfaced and I found myself intermittently reverting back to previously self-destructive ways – though on a much less regular or aggressive basis. I had developed an awareness of when I was operating from my fully resourced adult self, and similarly, when I wasn't - and whilst my recovery wasn't linear, I could more easily identify the personal and environmental triggers which invariably influenced my self-sabotage.

There remained an underbelly of emotional scar tissue, which had yet to be fully uncovered, explored and resolved.

> **"The cave you fear to enter, holds the treasure you seek."**
> **– Joseph Campbell**

Therapy and inner child work offer an invaluable source of inquiry for recognising personal triggers, traumas, and points of wounding - as well as the tools for dealing with same. In order to work toward a more evolved, elevated version of self, we very often need to first explore the original childhood wounds which led to the maladaptive and/or addictive response patterns, which present in adult life. Effective therapy teaches us the tools to identify and operate as our most capable, fully resourced adult selves - taking full responsibility for our lives and happiness, whilst having compassion for when our inner child becomes activated. Through acknowledging and embracing our fully integrated self (adult & child) we become better able to identify and operate from a place of wellness and self-care, whilst identifying limiting beliefs, triggers and behaviour patterns which inhibit forward progression.

Recovery and Maintenance

Whilst I'm now gratefully recovered and symptom free for several years, each day, I strive to continue maintaining a healthy balance and holistic approach to my body, food, weight and appearance. To this end, I incorporate daily practices of reflection, prayer, gratitude, meditation, exercise, eating healthily (but not overly so), thought management, affirmations, hobbies and maintaining positive connections. These combined practices, assist with my continued health and wellbeing in body, mind and spirit.

Regarding my physical recovery, I have maintained my weight and size pretty consistently for many years now (UK size 8, US size 2). I say this for the purpose of reassuring anyone who is currently struggling, that recovery is possible on every level – physical, psychological, emotional and spiritual. When we start to value, respect and cherish our body for the wonderful gift that it is, and stop treating it like a garbage can - it repays us by finding its own natural set point, without any undue force or pressure.

The Off-Days

Like most, I still have days and moments where I feel insecure and critical of my physical appearance and body - and on those days, I literally apply all the tricks of the trade! I use my breath, which is the fastest way to calm and regulate our nervous systems - to ground myself in present moment awareness. I then silence my inner critic and any negative thought flooding, with a variety of cognitive behaviour therapy (CBT), mindfulness, and compassion focused therapy (CFT) techniques.

Cognitive Behaviour Therapy seeks to establish the validity of negative thoughts - offering evidence to the contrary, whilst Compassion Focused Therapy gently and compassionately encourages the replacement of critical thoughts with positive statements of affirmation. Mindfulness brings us back to present moment awareness and gratitude for all that is in the here and now.

Additionally if needed, I journal, making a self-enquiry around what I need in order to feel better - which is usually not a new outfit as my mind or ego would have me believe, and instead something altogether more wholesome, e.g. taking a time-out, having a salt bath, listening to music, reading a book, taking time in nature, going for a run, meeting with friends, meditating, connecting with a loved one, fun and laughter!

The Journey

It's been a journey for me to fully internalise, that true beauty doesn't come from our external appearance, the numbers on the scale, or a specific clothes size. True and lasting beauty comes from a combination of self-care and well-being – from the kindness we extend to others, the spirit, attractiveness, buoyancy, humour and presence we exude in each and every moment, and the value we place on accepting, cherishing and expressing our unique, authentic, wonderful imperfect selves!

The Power of Words and Language

Anorexia, Bulimia, Body Dysmorphia, Binge-Eating Disorder, Orthorexia (obsession with healthy eating), Avoidant Restrictive Food Intake Disorder (avoiding/restricting to the point of obsession) are serious clinical issues which need to be acknowledged, addressed and comprehensively understood. The source of regular misinterpretation, shaming remarks such as "They look anorexic", "They look fat", "They're obsessed with their appearance" "They could do with eating a decent meal" "They could do with pulling away from the table" "If they stood beside a pole, you wouldn't see them", do little to assist the sufferer - whether stated directly or otherwise. If anything, such misinformed judgment merely exacerbates an already complex issue - further perpetuating a collective misunderstanding and prevailing ignorance in the wider domain. We need a greater, more compassionate awareness of the impact of harsh language when describing people's appearance - cognisant that if it's not kind, then it's not cool - and therefore, it's better left unsaid.

**"Opportunities to find deeper powers within ourselves
come, when life seems most challenging."
– Joseph Campbell**

Although difficult, I believe we learn and grow most as individuals through life's trials and adversities. This has been without doubt, the most raw and vulnerable chapter for me to write - however, in so doing, I hope that it will inspire others who have similarly suffered, or who currently do so in silence. Eating Disorders and Body Image Disturbances are serious complexities, which can lead to lifelong threatening physical, behavioural, emotional, psychological and social complications. It is difficult to quote reliable statistics regarding incidence and prevalence, for the very reason that many who suffer, do so in silence without seeking support. This is further perpetuated by the diet industry - a multi-billion euro/dollar enterprise, which thrives on making people feel insecure and worthless, because of their body weight and size.

"There is a crack in everything, that's how the light gets in."
– Leonard Cohen

In Japanese culture, 'Kintsugi', also known as 'golden repair' is the ancient art of repairing broken pottery by mending the areas of breakage with gold lacquer. Each area of breakage and repair is thought to be part of the history and uniqueness of the object - and therefore something to embrace rather than disguise. More than a mere aesthetic, this is part of the Japanese philosophy of embracing human flaws, understanding that each piece is more beautiful for having been broken.

In sharing this, I've had final closure on the shame and embarrassment I needlessly carried for years - even long after making a full recovery. We can never fully own or come into our true power if there's an aspect of ourselves we continue to reject, hide, silence or shame. By accepting ourselves as the scarred, imperfect, yet wonderful beings we are - who share many similar difficulties and life struggles along the way, there is a beauty and transcendence to that, which enables us to more fully understand and embrace ourselves - as well as each other.

> *"The quest for perfection our society demands, can leave the individual gasping for breath at every turn. This pressure inevitably extends into the way we look. Eating Disorders, whether it be anorexia or bulimia, show how an individual can turn the nourishment of the body into a painful attack on themselves, and they have at their core, a far deeper problem than mere vanity. From early childhood, many have felt they were expected to be perfect, but*

didn't feel they had the right to express their true feelings to those around them; feelings of guilt, of self revulsion and low personal esteem, creating in them a compulsion to dissolve like a disprin, and disappear. The illness they developed became their shameful friend. By focusing their energies on controlling their bodies, they found a refuge from having to face the more painful issues at the centre of their lives. Yes, people are dying from eating disorders, yet all of us can help prevent the seeds of this disease by developing as parents, teachers, family and friends. We have an obligation to care for our children in ways which clearly show our children that we value them. They in their turn will then learn how to value themselves, yet with greater awareness and more information, these people who are locked into a spiral of secret despair, can be reached before the dis-ease takes over their lives. I am certain the ultimate solution lies within the individual, but also with the help and patient nurturing given by you, the professionals, family and friends so that people suffering from eating disorders can find a better way of coping with their lives." (Diana, Princess of Wales, 27/4/1993)

For further information, consult www.bodywhys.ie

THE PSYCHOLOGY,
PHYSIOLOGY AND
IMPACT OF THOUGHT

Originating from the Book of Proverbs, "As a man thinks in his heart, so is he", the subject of thought has been widely researched and written about over the years. Thinking has a profound effect on our inner lives and outer world, and when we master the art of thought discipline, our inner and outer worlds change immeasurably. Cognitive Behaviour Therapy, Dialectical Behaviour Therapy, Compassion Focused Therapy, Acceptance and Commitment Therapy, Mindfulness and Meditation, are among the new wave therapies used to assist people with better thought management - the evidence of which leaves little doubt about the potent impact of thought on peoples' lives. What we give our attention to and think about and most, is essentially who we become.

Aligning Thought, Emotion and Action

Whilst most of the Twentieth Century was spent believing that the brain was fixed, static and immutable, recent years have identified the brain's plasticity - which essentially refers to the brain's ability to adapt, change and rewire. In his compelling book, 'Into the Magic Shop',

Neurosurgeon, Dr. James Doty, offers a modern-day account of neuro-plasticity and the symbiotic interplay of the heart and mind (Doty, 2016). Dr. Doty describes his journey through childhood, relaying his quest to discover the mysteries of the brain and secrets of the heart. He relays his journey and experiences from childhood - offering compelling evidence and credibility to the ancient wisdoms of visualisation, the power of intention, the potency of relaxation and healing power of compassion. Each practice immensely impact the brain's neurochemistry, and corresponding life experiences.

Thought impacts emotion, which impacts behaviour, and since 90% of our thoughts are reportedly repetitive (Luskin, 2012), it makes practical as well as psychological sense, to pay close attention to the mind software we use – upgrading accordingly. When the mind becomes corrupted due to thinking negative thoughts, the consequences are often debilitating. However, when the mind's infrastructure is upgraded to recognise, address and replace unsupportive thought systems with better thinking hygiene, our lives become exponentially better. This in turn exposes us to infinitely greater possibilities, imaginations and life experiences.

Dr. Doty believes change is facilitated when we commit to ensuring our thoughts, words, actions and intentions are aligned with purpose – and that they function together with compassion and integrity. This comes through recognising that mind and heart do not function as separate entities - rather they are part of a unified intelligence, connected through the vagus nerve. Before taking an action therefore or making a decision, we benefit most from pausing first to engage the heart, and then engaging the mind. In so doing, we are more likely to inform action which is motivated from a place of compassion which is for the greater good - as distinct from self-interest alone. Nothing is achieved by simply willing it to be - action is required, and when action is supported by integrity and purpose, this leads to the highest form of goal attainment, manifestations, and actions for the greater good. (Doty, 2016)

Focus and Goal Activation

We are creatures of habit and very often favour the easiest possible route to attainment and success - with the least amount of effort. In our mind's eye, we desire our outer lives to match our inner vision, yet so often we're unwilling to complete the action steps necessary to achieve the desired outcome. This is the difference between having lofty, aspirational goals, and actually working and taking the required steps toward the attainment or manifestation of such goals. Books, podcasts, uplifting quotes, attending the a-z of personal development, and watching inspirational online content is great, however these remain largely time depleting activities unless the information ingested is followed up with appropriate action steps.

So, whilst sitting alone on a mountain top meditating all day may be relaxing and of benefit, it's unlikely to transfer most effectively to real life situations - where we've to deal with daily distractions, irritants and triggers occurring on the daily. The same applies to sitting, visualising and manifesting a better life in one's room all day – goal attainment requires movement, focus, direction, purpose, and real-life stress testing! We are unlikely to turn conscious thought into conscious achievement therefore, without the necessary, appropriate, conscious action.

Start where you are, use what you have, do what you can

It is said that knowledge is potential power - depending on how we apply it to our lives. If we aspire to greater heights psychologically, physically, intellectually, emotionally and spiritually, we must be prepared to do the work required to effect change in each of these areas. Motivational guru, author, and world renowned speaker, Anthony Robbins, describes this process as holding ourselves accountable to a higher standard of excellence – whether this is at work, in our personal relationships, romantic lives, physical fitness, health and finances. Robbins suggests that it is only in holding ourselves to a higher standard of excellence, and by becoming personally aware of what this means to us individually, that we

#DrDee

begin to effect change in our lives (Robbins, 2001). This doesn't have to be necessarily ground breaking, monumental change – small, daily, incremental, consistent change, can equally have a significant impact on our output and confidence.

Maintaining High Standards Vs Perfectionism

Whilst holding ourselves to a high standard is commendable, this should not be confused with perfectionism. Being perfectionist is the fastest way to feeling inadequate, disempowered, fearful and self-critical - emotions which are the exact opposite to feeling good and accomplishing goals. So instead of starting and never finishing several projects - begin one, and focus on seeing it through to the end, however slowly. This could be anything from baking a cake to tackling laundry, writing a book, to submitting a proposal – "Done, is better than perfect."

Mind and Thought Power

Philosopher and Poet, Ralph Waldo Emerson proposed, "A man is what he thinks about all day long - how could he be anything else?", whilst Roman Emperor and Philosopher, Marcus Aurelius, summed up his life philosophy in eight words, "Our life is what our thoughts make it".

A positive mind-set is powerful and assists not only in our personal relationships, but in our relationship with self. If we think fearful thoughts we will most likely feel anxious and fearful; if we think miserable thoughts, we will probably feel gloomy and miserable; if we think failure thoughts, we are more likely to fail, if we think angry thoughts, we are more likely to harbour rage and resentment toward others.

Energy flows where attention goes, so in order to change our feelings and circumstances, we must first begin to think in a different way.

Choosing Thoughts

It is impossible to have a healthy mind-set with optimal output, if we continue to think in defeatist, ruminative ways. Such unsupportive thinking styles, are destructive - both to ourselves and to those around us. Am I suggesting we adopt a 'Polyanna attitude' instead – feigning ever-present positivity, and bypassing life's realities, difficulties and misfortunes? Absolutely not. I am however suggesting that even in times of trial, we strive to the best of our ability, for a more accepting, optimistic attitude - refusing to allow burdens, defeat, negative people, situations and circumstances to gain the upper hand and weigh us down. Full acceptance of an event or experience means giving up the hope of it having being any different - surrendering to the idea of what is, versus what we would've wished it to be.

In each moment, we are 100% responsible for how we choose to think and respond to people, circumstances and events therefore - which is something we often forget, somehow believing that we are instead at the mercy of external situations, people and our emotions.

We cannot choose what happens to us in life, however we can always choose our response

So what are the mechanics involved in choosing the thoughts that best serve us in our daily lives, as opposed to those that heighten or exacerbate anxiety and stress? Attention creates the ripened conditions and environment necessary for change to occur in our brains. The more attention we give to a particular thought, the more it amplifies and grows. This is good when our focus of attention is on healthy, evolved thoughts - but not so good in the instance of toxic, unhealthy ones.

When the seeds of toxicity are planted and watered, they take root in powerfully destructive ways. Unless observed in the first instance and weeded out, negative thoughts grow and bear bad fruit in our lives as well as in our relationships.

The importance of cultivating a positive thought life

In James Allen's 1902 iconic book, 'As a man thinketh', Allen offers a brief account of the importance of mastering the human mind. In it he writes, "Man is made or unmade by himself". He proposes that you cannot choose your circumstances, but you can choose the thoughts you ascribe to circumstances. He suggests fate and luck have little hand to play in one's journey to success - rather the changing of our internal thoughts and perceptions.

Our thoughts, similar to the maintenance of a garden, may be positively coaxed and groomed - or on the contrary, allowed to grow wildly without purpose, boundary or direction. Allen describes this process as becoming the master gardener of one's soul - the director of one's life - pulling and weeding redundant damaging thoughts, and cultivating positive ones instead. Thoughts are likened to seeds - the good bearing wisdom, the bad leading to unruliness and destruction. (Allen, 2003)

Negative Effect of Destructive Thoughts

"But how am I supposed to accept x or stop thinking about y? - I was wronged in that situation, and I'm entitled to feel angry/sad/resentful/wronged."

We are absolutely entitled to our emotions - it can be incredibly difficult to let go of unjust pain, suffering or any other juxtaposing situation in which we find, or have found ourselves at different times. However, if holding stubbornly to a particular thought or grudge becomes damaging to our personal health, whilst the other person obliviously carries on - it is to our detriment, not theirs. We're essentially allowing them to live rent-free in our minds - perhaps believing that if we don't nurse and continually replay a particular wound or injustice, that we're somehow letting them, "off the hook". We may even believe the situation won't get better without giving it our full twenty four-seven, constant negative attention.

#DrDee

The impact of Anger and Resentment

Holding onto anger, hurt or resentment doesn't make it go away - on the contrary, it invariably makes the pain we suffer feel worse. The more attention we give to negative, resentful thoughts and emotions, the more toxically threatening to our health they become, and the worse we feel. Buddha believed that holding on to anger is like holding a hot coal with the intention of throwing it at someone else – we're the ones who ultimately get burned.

Prepare, activate, accept

We prepare for life as it naturally unfolds - not from forcing our perceived ideal of how we think it should be. Much of life is beyond our control after all, and human suffering is both indiscriminate and inevitable. Irrespective of ethnicity, race, gender, intellectual ability, financial, social, physical, political or educational standing - we will each experience suffering and struggle at some point. Therefore, since we can't control it, the only rational response is to accept life on life's terms - focusing on adapting our response to challenging situations, people and circumstances as best we can.

Choosing Thoughts Consciously

Whilst we have little control over the thoughts that enter our minds, we have absolute power over the attention or air time to which we give each one. For many, this is a revelation, and often one which is met with rebuttal. 75-98% of the illnesses that plague us as humans are a direct result of our thought lives (Leaf, 2015). We are creatures of habit and our thinking patterns are no different. Therefore, the concept of having the ability to choose our thoughts in the same way as we choose our clothes, seems absurd. People often report to strongly believing that they are powerlessly and uncontrollably at the mercy of their thoughts, and so it takes time and practiced discipline to facilitate the evolvement of more supportive thought hygiene – which is often helped by practices such as meditation and relaxation.

Automatic Negative Thoughts (ANT's)

Negative thinking styles result in a flood of ANT's camping-out in our minds. ANT's – automatic negative thoughts - referred to formally in Cognitive Behaviour Therapy as negative automatic thoughts (NAT's). As the name suggests, NAT's occur unconsciously and automatically - resulting in an infestation of automatic negative thoughts – ANT's in our minds. This is not helped by the fact that as humans, we have a tendency toward a negative bias, i.e. we are more automatically predisposed to viewing things in a negative way. We view the glass as half empty instead of half full, or a combination of half empty and half full. We focus on the 10% lost instead of the 90% gained. We underscore the one negative comment amidst a sea of positives. We notice someone's one annoying personality trait, as opposed to admiring their many positives.

It takes time, attention, focused discipline, persistence - and in many cases, the help of a skilled therapist, to firstly become aware, and then to tackle automatic negative thoughts. When we become equipped with the skills or 'know how' to recruit automatic negative thought (ANT) eaters, i.e. strategies to help us to deal with negative thought patterns - we are better positioned to respond to life's challenges and to connect with self and others in a more positive, affirming manner.

Cognitive Reframing

As referred to above, one of the approaches used for dealing with negative thought patterns, is Cognitive Behaviour Therapy (CBT) (Beck, 1967). CBT requires us to firstly become aware of our negative automatic thoughts, to catch them as they occur, and to then challenge their validity and reliability. In many cases what we find by doing this, is that the thoughts we most repetitively think about, have absolutely no business taking up any space in our minds! There is generally no evidence supporting their truth and they generally serve no value for us to ruminate upon.

Therefore, similar to a case being thrown out in a court of law, we need to examine the validity and truth of our thoughts and beliefs - establishing reliable evidence to support their continued occupancy in our minds, and ridding ourselves of invalid, redundant ones. For example, someone may have the persistent thought that they are not clever, yet when you probe the evidence to support that belief, there are countless examples of how bright and intelligent the person is.

Belief Systems

Sometimes, we unknowingly adopt the belief systems of other people who have been strong influences in our lives, e.g. parents, teachers, and other childhood authoritative key figures. Adult beliefs such as, "My teacher in third class/grade told me I was stupid", or "My father told me I would never amount to anything", "My mother told me I wasn't wanted", serve no purpose to ruminate upon, other than to cause extreme mental and emotional distress. It's important to note therefore, the penetrative impact of holding persistent negative thoughts and beliefs in our minds without remission.

Maladaptive belief patterns very often become so deeply ingrained, that they cause people to repeat the same ineffective thinking and behaviour patterns over and over - leading to the same negative personal actions, implications and consequences. Left unchecked, this can result in a host of secondary difficulties, including addiction and/or substance misuse, anxiety, social isolation, relationship difficulties, or any other maladaptive thinking pattern response.

Core Beliefs

In Psychology, we refer to the belief systems we hold about ourselves, other people, and the world, as core beliefs. Core beliefs are essentially what we believe to be true - deep down, below our surface level thoughts. Unless brought to conscious level awareness, core beliefs can ineffectively determine how we perceive, interpret, and respond to life and the

#DrDee

world. The assistance of a Psychologist, Counsellor, Psychotherapist, Life Coach or Mentor therefore, may again help to uncover, challenge, and transform maladaptive core beliefs.

Welcoming Light and Dark Emotions

In Rumi's eloquent poem 'The Guest House', he speaks of welcoming both good and bad thoughts and emotions. He encourages us to embrace, without judgment - the shame, the anger, the sadness, the jealousy, the darkness, the fear, and to treat each of them honourably - as we would a guest, since they have been sent to us as our teacher.

The poem explores the position that by virtue of our humanity, two opposing forces are in constant opposition with one another. As a mirror holds two sides, we are each comprised of light and dark, however somewhere along the way we internalised the belief that it's not ok or acceptable to have a shadow side. From the time we were children, we were taught "to be good"; "to be nice" - the consequence of which lead to us often being too ashamed to admit the mere existence of negative or dark thoughts.

It's human to sometimes think, feel and act in unbecoming ways - it is part of our flawed, imperfect nature. Ironically, this makes for far more interesting characters in movies and works of fiction - however in real life, this generally isn't the case. When we become aware of an exposed aspect of our shadow self, it's best to acknowledge and take corrective action as early as possible – before it becomes a greater source of distress to self and others. This is not to harshly judge oneself, rather – as Rumi recommends, to note the presence of a less desirable emotion, and its effects.

In the words of Author, John Steinbeck, "Our human foibles don't negate our goodness or our desire for betterment, but rather, provide both the fuel for it and the yardstick by which we measure our moral progress. (Steinbeck, 1941).

"We must feel it to heal it"

Whilst it's perfectly normal to feel the occurrence of darker emotions, it is equally important we don't remain stuck there for too long. Our initial task is therefore to recognise and identify when our thoughts and/or behaviour becomes compromised, negative or weakened in some way, and to make efforts to correspondingly correct and address as appropriate.

Everything holds a finite cycle - including our emotions, so instead of judging, suppressing or negating the effect or felt presence of darker emotion, a healthier response is to allow it to pass through freely in an unforced, cloud-like manner. This is the method purported in Acceptance and Commitment Therapy (Hayes et al, 2016) where thoughts and emotions are welcomed and given the space for exploration and acknowledgment. Recognised as transient messengers, we get to witness, examine, understand and reframe our thoughts and emotions through the eyes of a curious observer - as opposed to a critical judge.

Neuroplasticity

Much has been written in recent years, on the subject of Neuroplasticity. What and how we choose to think, activates and changes the structure of our brains - which is ultimately to our benefit or demise (Leaf, 2010, '13). Brain plasticity demonstrates that we can literally reframe and rewire neural pathways, through repeated thought patterns and corresponding behaviours. The way we think impacts either positively or negatively on the health of our brains and bodies, and whilst the basic brain structures are the same for all of us, the connections between the nerve tissues and cells are constantly changing each time we think or re-experience something. We can strengthen these nerve connections in a positive or negative direction - depending on how we repeatedly choose to think. In this sense, the brain anatomy and connective architecture differs dramatically from one individual to the next - depending on their thought lives.

Thoughts under the Microscope

"I'm too young for this job, they will never take on anyone as young or as inexperienced as me".

If we were to put a positive reframe on this thought, it would appear something like the following:

"I'm young and vibrant. I'll bring new knowledge and fresh ideas to this company who will be lucky to have me as an employee".

Or ....

"I'm young and vibrant with great ideas - what's to stop me from setting up my own company!"

Each statement occupies the same core belief - being too young or inexperienced for the job. However, the core belief in each, is vastly different. In the first example, the language used confirms a negative self-fulfilling prophecy of failure expectancy - whilst in the examples that follow, the initial limiting belief system is re-framed with optimistic, self-affirming statements of belief.

Brain Training

It is possible to train our brains to think of any life situation in a similarly life affirming way. In fact, the more we train and focus on nourishing our brain health, the quicker it adapts and re-shapes into a stronger, more resilient working mass.

This may be likened to building muscle mass in our bodies at the gym. Time, consistency, dedication, motivation, training and rest are required to build bodily muscle fibre. Similarly, the recruitment of specific brain pathways are required to strengthen the connective tissue in the brain - which over time, allows us to think, act and make decisions more effectively and efficiently.

Brain-Body Strength and Connection

1) Recognition of the improvements we desire. Conducting an honest appraisal of self – where we're at currently, and what we'd like to transform.
2) Acknowledgment of the work necessary to gain enhanced strength, conditioning and transformation.
3) Commitment to the work, discipline, dedication, accountability and reflection required to achieve the elevated result.
4) Awareness that although muscle fibres cannot be observed by the physical eye as they are physically being broken down, torn and transformed - recalibration and reorganising is happening beneath the surface during rest - the longer we persevere, the more satisfying, sustaining and visible our results will be to self and others.
5) Once change is observed with improvements to physical, emotional, mental, psychological and social wellbeing - this translates to better health, enhanced wellbeing and greater resilience and connection.

Neuroplasticity and Inter-Connectivity

Plasticity does not occur in isolation. Positive change in one area of the brain tends to lead to positive changes in others too. This ability of the brain to adapt and change is supported by the evidence that where one brain system changes, the systems connected to it change also (Arnheim, 1979 in Leaf, 2010). This may account for the cascading-effect observed, when we start to experience success in one area of our lives which then reverberates to other areas too. How we do one thing essentially becomes how we do everything.

The opposite is often the case however also. When we foster toxic, negative, inflammatory thoughts, these infiltrate the connective brain tissue network - which in turn disrupts and corrupts our cycle of thought. The development of the brain is therefore largely under our control. We are not victims of our biology or environment - although both influence our tendencies in any one particular direction. Our brains are designed with an ability to renew, restructure, redirect and rewire. The traditional view therefore - that past behaviour is the best predictor of future behaviour, holds less weight, since brain studies have shown the incredible plasticity of the brain (Leaf, 2021). This suggests that who we were before, does not determine who we can become in the future.

Steps for dealing with Negative Thoughts

We can make a conscious choice to either perseverate on negative thoughts, or we can choose to interrupt the negative cycle.

The following may offer assistance with this process:

1) Notice and acknowledge the thought as it appears. Refrain from judging or criticising the thought - simply acknowledge its presence and allow it to pass through (use the visual of a moving cloud if helpful).
2) If the thought persists and you find yourself obsessing - challenge the validity or rational basis of the thought. Journal/meditate/pray about it, or use whatever practice you find helpful to gain further clarity regarding the thought rumination.
3) Open and engage the heart. This will allow a more expansive, compassionate, non-judgmental, and less ego-driven perspective to emerge.
4) Question the usefulness of maintaining the thought in its current form, considering the impact on your wellbeing and relationships with others. Is the thought helping or hindering?
5) If the thought is hurting or not serving you, make a conscious choice to reframe, reconceptualise, reconcile, transform, transmute or dispense with the thought for something more affirming.

#DrDee

Setting Intentions and Affirmations

Setting our minds to the highest possible frequency can be positively facilitated by establishing a supportive morning routine. Upon waking, train yourself to set your thoughts and intentions to the highest possible frequency - which may be assisted using affirmations such as:

> "I'm thankful to be alive and well"
>
> "I am safe and secure in myself and in my body"
>
> "Today will be a great day"
>
> "I am open and receptive to all the abundance The Universe/Life/God has to offer"

Follow with any other positive affirmations or declarations of gratitude you wish, and then visualise yourself in each segment of your day - thinking, speaking, acting and listening in the poised, mindful, intentional manner you aspire toward.

This better prepares us for dealing with problems and challenges as they arise, and whilst it won't miraculously guarantee a problem free day - it will help set our minds toward a more enlightened focus, enabling us to re-calibrate more easily when problems arise.

Segment Intending

Author and Speaker, Esther Hicks, refers to the concept of 'Segment Intending', which involves intending each segment of our day - instead of mindlessly allowing triggers and our environment to unconsciously dictate how we act or respond to situations. Hicks suggests we use the segment intending approach, to reorient ourselves and get our thoughts back on track at any time of day - regardless of how derailed they have become.

#DrDee

For example, we may be resetting to return to an original task - or pivoting from a lone task to a group task - or about to meet a new client - or entering a potentially challenging meeting. Whatever the case, we can take a moment to realign, become conscious of our thoughts and energy, and consciously intend how we would like our next segment or meeting to flow. The more we become consciously aware of our thoughts, behaviours and emotions, the less likely we are to think and react in habitual, destructive, unconscious patterns.

Reaction vs Response

In Professor Steve Peter's book, "The Chimp Paradox", he refers to high expressed emotion and associated rash action - as stemming from thoughts coming from the limbic or emotional brain (Peters, 2012). Although all areas of the brain are interconnected, the limbic brain is primarily responsible for our emotional or stress response. It activates the fight, flight, feign or freeze response - causing us to react impulsively in the moment.

The pre-frontal-cortex (PFC), located to the front of the brain, adopts a more paternal role within the brain structure - therefore exercising control over planning, decision making, organising and insight. When conditioned over time - through consistent reflective practices such as mindfulness, meditation, yoga and relaxation, we are more likely to respond to situations with greater strength, diplomacy and higher order thinking.

The PFC & Limbic System

The limbic brain and pre frontal cortex need to be in harmonious connection with each other - to keep our nervous systems calm, and to effectively regulate our emotions (Amen, 2020). Stress can disrupt the circuitry between the pre-frontal cortex and the limbic system, releasing cortisol which causes inflammation. Such inflammation impacts our ability to think well and to make good decisions, which may be further

#DrDee

exacerbated by poor sleep, ingestion of highly processed/fatty foods, excess sugar, refined carbohydrates, lack of exercise, excessive digital exposure, decreased time in nature, lack of human connection, and an absence of gratitude (Amen; Perlmutter, 2019).

What can we do to minimise inflammation in the brain, improve the limbic-frontal connection, activate positive neuroplasticity, and improve our overall brain health?

1) What we give our attention to is ultimately who we become, so pay close attention to daily thoughts and thinking patterns. Take corrective action in the case of automatic negative thoughts and rash, impulsive reactions.

2) Exercise and get active. This will activate and enable the secretion of endorphins - our body's natural painkillers, which will lead to better feeling thoughts and overall better mental and physical health.

3) Develop a brain that makes good choices and decisions by practicing the pause. Actively engage the insightful pre frontal cortex - instead of remaining in the reactive limbic zone.

4) Our decisions are a reflection of our brain health, so pay conscious attention to reducing body and brain inflammation - which will lead to better thinking and decision making. Reducing intake of fatty, sugary, highly processed and refined foods - instead replacing them with colourful brain foods such as blueberries, bananas, spinach, and avocados (which are loaded with antioxidants), will nourish the brain, improve concentration and reduce inflammation (Amen, 2019).

5) Spending as little as 20 minutes in nature has been shown to lower cortisol - the hormone responsible for stress. Stress disables our ability to make good decision, causing a disruption of the circuitry between the pre frontal cortex and the limbic or emotional brain. Spending time in nature redresses this and fosters a healthy connection between the pre-frontal and limbic brain – resulting in less stress, better thoughts, and better decision making overall (Amen, 2020).

6) Have an attitude of gratitude. Since it is difficult to be irritated and grateful at the same time, begin a gratitude journal. This will foster appreciation for what is working well in our lives - as it stimulates the brain to look for the positive, whilst releasing a steady flow of dopamine and serotonin, which are the feel good hormones associated with lowered stress.

7) Spend less time on social media and more time in nature and connecting with people in the physical world. Social media can foster narcissism, stress, and disconnection from others in those who are susceptible to spending several unproductive hours on-line. *Consider David Perlmutter's 'Test of Time Tool' for examining online tendencies (Perlmutter, 2019)

8) Meditation as a scientifically proven way of activating the pre frontal cortex (Amen, 2019) which will lead to enhanced decision making and less reactivity in triggering situations.

9) Foster a brain that chooses the fruit instead of the pastry, through repeated conscious thought conditioning.

"Our habits will either make or break us.
We become what we repeatedly do."
~ Sean Covey

FRIENDSHIPS AND RELATIONSHIPS

"Nobody thinks of longevity as adding friends to our lives, but really putting the effort into creating that group of three, four or five people who really nourish you, is arguably the most powerful thing you can do to add years to your life." (Buettner, 2019). The importance of friendships and choosing our relations mindfully cannot be underestimated. Author Jim Rohn, proposed that we are the average of the five people with whom we spend our most time (Rohn, 2013), and whilst genuine connection and concern for the wider community has been shown to greatly impact our mental and physical health (Thoits, 2011), who we allow into our immediate circle has a significant bearing on how we show up in the world. Where we place our attention, and who we hang out with, is essentially who we become.

Relationships and Life

Social connections play a protective role in maintaining a robust mental and emotional framework, so although we may not always feel like reaching out to others, the benefits of doing so have been extensively documented (Santos, 2021). We live in a fast paced society, and the pressure of keeping on top of daily demands - like meeting deadlines, smashing goals, achieving targets, and well… you know the usual stuff of being an adoring partner, amazing parent, model offspring, stellar employee, conscientious student, successful entrepreneur, thoughtful friend, kind sibling, regular fitness enthusiast, domestic goddess, perfect clothes hanger, hip content producer, total babe magnet and well, general all-round sex god! The standards we place upon ourselves are often impossibly high, yet we regularly neglect to practice self-care – the very core of what enables us to inhabit and extend ourselves healthily.

"No man is an island"

Like most successfully cultivated connections, meaningful relationships are built upon solid foundations of time, attention, connection, care, trust, kindness, respect, freedom, fun and open communication. As humans, we were designed to live in community and communion with one another - succinctly captured by the phrase "No man is an island" (Donne, 1642). The simple act of being in the company of people we enjoy - evokes a sense of ease, understanding, shared connection, fun, and a feeling of being less burdened by the struggles and demands of everyday life. We were born to connect with each other - to share, to love, to laugh, to help each other along the way, to celebrate each other's achievements, mourn each other's losses, exchange stories, and add the sparkle to the everyday mundane.

But have we become somewhat estranged from our inherent tribal nature? Has our preoccupation with being independent and amassing materialism and wealth, replaced our humble roots as hunter-gatherers? British Activist and Writer, Russel Brand - following some of the positive inter-connectedness which were reported during the peak of the Covid-19 pandemic, posed the question on his Instagram grid, "How can we organise society in a way that is conducive to our evolved nature - living in smaller communities, inter-connected with one another, and aligned with our inner and outer nature - forming purposeful, co-operative, collaborative relationships?" (Brand, 2021)

Journalist and Author, Johann Hari riffs on a similar theme in his international best-seller, 'Lost Connections'. Quoted by the British Journal of General Practice as one of the most important texts of recent years (Bransby, 2018), Hari documents his extensive travels and global conversations with people – proposing a link between people's experience of depression and anxiety, with external stressors such as disconnection, loneliness, and work based dissatisfaction. Hari suggests that the world's growing levels of depression and anxiety are related to the disconnected, consumer based culture we live in today, and suggests unconventional treatments such as community based volunteer projects and non-hierarchical workplaces as alternative options toward improving human connections and mental health. (Hari, 2018)

Life is better when we're afforded the opportunity to choose in accordance with what feels aligned to our particular values and preferences - and whilst Johann Hari's suggestions may require additional support in more extreme situations, e.g. in the case of an acute psychiatric or psychotic presentation (where someone may require the appropriate medical and/or pharmacological interventions), his observations are hugely significant in the overall context and conversation regarding contemporary progressive treatment options, and service provision for mental health.

Choosing Friends

Dating back to pre-historic times, humans have always sought out like-minded people - to feel connected, respected, accepted and loved. Our choice of friends is often reflective of our most highly valued human qualities, likes, characteristics and traits. We generally gravitate toward the people who "get us", and with whom we feel a shard affinity - and with whom the feeling appears mutual. Therefore, when choosing friends and establishing relationships, it's not only important to establish connections, but to do so discerningly.

In order to expand our consciousness, it's also worth considering opening our hearts and minds to people who offer more diverse perspectives to that of our own. Whilst such relationships may not necessarily mature to friendship level, by becoming engaged with different conversations and perspectives, this enables our mind-set and world view to be broadened – which is never a bad thing!

Shared Values

Adopting a wide lens perspective - among other benefits, leaves us better placed to make informed choices regarding our likes, dislikes, and core values. Core values are key to any relationship, and generally play a major role in its success or demise. Whilst we may admire certain differences in others - seeing them as adding spice or novelty to a relationship connection, if someone's core values are completely at odds with our own - or become so over time, this can result in challenges, or the relationship dissolving completely.

An example may be where two people have been friends for a long time, and realise that as their paths have diverged, so too have their values. Perhaps one person continues to enjoy the party lifestyle, whilst the other has become more family oriented and no longer shares the same enthusiasm for social nights out. This may result in a parting of ways - as one or both parties struggle to reclaim common ground. On the other hand, the friendship may deepen and stand the test of time, if both parties are open and accepting of each other's evolving paths. One of the keys to sustaining a successful relationship in the long-term therefore, is clear communication and focusing on the relationship strengths and valued qualities - as opposed to honing in on apparent differences.

"With great friendship comes great responsibility."

In order to have good relationships, we must ourselves embody that which we most value and wish to receive. For example, if we like being heard - we need to practice being a good listener; If we value kindness and empathy - we need to practice being kind and understanding toward others; If we enjoy being remembered - we need to practice thoughtfulness; and if we like it when someone responds quickly to a text - we need to be equally prompt in our response style...

These are just some of the examples which can lead to finger pointing and blame assignation in relationships - where standards and expectations are not met. Relationship harmony is a two-way street, and since we can never be responsible for changing another's behaviour, it's best to remain focused on changing our own. Thus, when relationships expose our less than proud or polished side - as they often do, instead of immediately blaming the other person, we might instead pause to reflect on our own behaviour - taking appropriate ownership and responsibility accordingly.

Respecting Difference

For a relationship to work, there needs to be an acceptance of each other's personality and character traits. By rising above the idea that everyone is compelled to act in a certain manner - usually in a way that most closely resembles how we believe we would behave in a similar situation, enhances our relationship connections significantly. The first rule of thumb in close relationships is therefore to figure out what our deal breakers are. What are our absolute "no, no's"? What do we maybe dislike, but are willing to accept or tolerate? For example, someone lying or being disloyal may be a complete deal breaker, however their tendency to be forgetful or untidy might be something we can overlook.

As adults, people are free to act as they choose - it is not our responsibility to correct or impose our expectations regarding how we think grown adults "should" or "should not" behave. We can certainly express respectful dislike, however it is not our responsibility to try to change, manipulate or control another's behaviour. If we think of how difficult it is to change something within ourselves, we will have some measure of what's involved in trying to change another. The responsibility therefore lies within each one of us - to mindfully address what needs to be acknowledged within ourselves - perhaps via a change in attitude, a decision to let go of something, or to overlook a particular irritant. In so doing, we very often effect positive change in the relationship, as a by-product of reframing our own perspective. The primary work therefore happens within ourselves -not with trying to control the behaviour of another.

Respect for Self, Respect for Others

In instances where we reach a complete impasse with regard to behaviour we deem as completely unacceptable or inappropriate within a relationship, this needs careful consideration. Like a budding flower which requires the right soil, space and nourishment to fully thrive and bloom; we similarly need key ingredients for our friendships, relationships and we ourselves, to blossom. Pay attention to those who are persistently unavailable when times are tough, and equally those who appear unable to clap when things are good - certain folk are better able to support and empathise when we're struggling, though sadly lack the capacity to be happy when we're celebrating or having a shining moment.

No matter how significant or long-standing a relationship, value yourself enough to walk away - or at the very least take time out, if you're experiencing jealous, unhealthy, unsupportive, neglectful, resentful, or toxic energies in a relationship. Seek out like-minded individuals instead - who value you with extended warmth, acknowledgment, reciprocity, positivity, kindness and respect. This will weaken and diminish any previously held feelings of guilt, shame, fear or self-doubt - emotions frequently instigated and riled by jealous, unhealthy energies.

> **"Everything that irritates us about others can lead us to a greater understanding of ourselves."**
> **- Carl Jung**

Becoming conscious of what we respond to most positively in others, offers insight to our preferred personality traits. Similarly, an awareness of our triggers, red flags and negative reactions - as captured by Jung's quote above, teaches us much about ourselves also. When we become curious about our reactions to the characteristics or behaviour patterns we find most irritating in others - we gain infinite wisdom and understanding about ourselves. If we are brave enough to examine who we perceive as our adversaries therefore, they become investigative parts of our own hidden, shadow personalities.

Giving and Receiving Feedback

Feedback is an effective, though often double-edged sword. It can be useful in relationships if offered respectfully - however it's also a risk, as we can never fully predict the outcome of how our feedback will be received. As feedback givers, we have the opportunity to express our truth instead of harbouring resentment or ill-feeling. This offers the benefit of keeping our relationships fluid – allowing the lines of communication to remain open.

As feedback receivers, we get to hear how the other person is experiencing us - which depending on our level of insight and self-awareness, may or may not be difficult to internalise. If feedback is offered by someone we trust in a respectful manner, and we are brave enough to put our egos to one side in considering their message, we have the potential to learn and evolve exponentially as humans - as well as in our relationships.

Important considerations when offering feedback

- Verbalise the intention of the discussion with the other person in advance, and ask if it's a good time for them to have the conversation
- Assume a calm relaxed state, with the intention to heal and resolve - not wound
- If the conversation becomes heated or argumentative, it may be wise to re-convene at a later time
- Avoid the use of excessive alcohol or drugs when having conversations of a sensitive nature

Life and Death are in the Power of the Tongue

Since our internal conversation is reflected onto pretty much everyone and everything we come into contact, it makes sense to pay close attention to the primary conversation we are having with ourselves. Once spoken, words cannot be rescinded, and thus it is our responsibility to recognise that our internal dialogue sets the tone for every other extended communication in our lives. Words have immense power and are most effective when chosen in a conscious, respectful manner. Therefore, although we may at times, have to deliver a harsh message - our manner of delivery is critical in how the message is received - and the ensuing impact on the relationship.

For example, if we're triggered by someone who shows up late, we can avoid reacting in a way that will stifle the tone of the meeting or compromise the relationship - by remaining calm. Instead of greeting the person with a punishing expression, sarcastic remark or vowing internally to make a similar late pay-back appearance - we might instead consider that such micro aggressions or any other form of passive aggressiveness, will further compromise the relationship connection.

With this - or any other triggering situation, we are more likely to achieve a better outcome by modelling the behaviour we most desire. Thus, if the desired behaviour is punctuality - we ourselves are best placed to show up on time, intending the best possible outcome for the meeting. If for whatever reason the other person falls short of this expectation, instead of becoming critical, judgmental or passive aggressive - we might instead respectfully enquire as to the reason why the behaviour may be persistently presenting.

e.g. "I'm sure it's not intentional (demonstrates empathy), but is there a reason you find it difficult to be here on time?" (non-threatening enquiry vs immediate accusation)

Wait for response....

#DrDee

Follow with, "I appreciate you're busy and have important things going on (demonstrates understanding), however when you show up late (action) it makes me feel like you think my time is less valuable than yours" (impact of action on self vs making value judgment on the other).

In this example, we are calmly seeking to establish the reason for the late behaviour. We are not labelling the person in any disrespectful or derogatory way, we are simply naming the behaviour and stating how it makes us feel. Thus, instead of shaming, blaming and inflaming the situation, we are seeking to establish clarity - by demonstrating a willingness to hear the other person's reasoning, yet maintaining a personal boundary, i.e "I'm not ok with you persistently showing up late".

This open, honest communication style, is more likely to evoke a calm discussion ensuing with ultimate resolve, as opposed to shutting down the channels of communication, and potentially causing further relationship fracture.

It is therefore possible to relay the same message - in two very different ways, and although we may not always achieve the desired outcome, we can come away from the situation feeling proud for having remained calm and respectful. The old sticks and stones adage therefore holds little weight - language and words have immense power!

Feeling Triggered?

If feeling triggered and wanting to lash out toward another, the following steps might be useful:

- Pause and take deep breaths (e.g. Box Breathing – inhale for five, hold for five, exhale for five).
- Place your hand on your heart and ask yourself, "What's showing up for me emotionally right now, that's making me want to speak or act out in this way?"

- Ask what you can do for yourself to calm and re-regulate the nervous system? e.g. further deep breaths, humming, taking time out, connecting with higher self, and asking for guidance.
- Use the fast forward technique to forward play to a future time or event where you have said what you're tempted to say. How will you feel? What is the potential impact to the relationship?
- Take time out to recalibrate and reset. Revisit when feeling more composed
- Sleep on it!

Setting Boundaries

People often conceptualise boundaries as a way of keeping people out - when boundaries may be thought of as a respectful way of keeping people in. Boundaries establish the rules and demarcations of healthy relationships - and with these in place, we're better equipped to understand and navigate the many extended relationships we have in our lives – from personal to professional and everything in-between. Boundaries begin and end with us. We set the tone and the markers, for what we will or won't accept, and when we remain firm in this - there is less likelihood of judgment or offence being taken, as people know exactly where they stand.

Setting and maintaining healthy boundaries can be tricky territory for people who despair at the idea of "real talks", or for those who associate being assertive with conflict or confrontation. This can lead to suppression of innermost feelings and desires - in a bid to please others or to not appear rude. Left unchecked, this "disease to please" may result in an inability to question, say no, assert a personal preference, express an opinion or belief, or state already existing plans. This occurs due to fear of being negatively judged, criticised, inadvertently punished, isolated, exiled, perceived or abandoned. Left unchecked, this pleasing affliction may become a running theme behind every choice, decision and conversation ever had.

Respectful boundaries bypass the need for ignoring, ghosting, excluding, minimising, bitching, belittling, gossiping, gaslighting, controlling, manipulating - or any other behaviour which threatens or compromises a relationship. Boundaries are there to help, not hinder - and when our boundaries are clear, this facilitates open honest communication and discussion - without fear of repercussion, gaslighting, or reprisal. Respectful boundaries do not require us to become ball busters, drama queens or to be in a perpetual state of offence, bitterness or pride. Rather, they allow us to hold a deep commitment and respect for what feels inherently right, and to communicate this in a respectful manner. We do this, whilst holding space - though not necessarily agreeing with others' values, opinions and standards.

One of my favourite sayings, quoted regularly by Oprah is, "We teach people how to treat us". What we permit is ultimately what persists and sets the tone for every relationship we have in our lives – whether family, friendships, acquaintances, romantic, work or otherwise. If someone knows they will get away with something - once enabled, they will continue to operate in this manner. It is incumbent on us therefore, to establish healthy boundaries from the outset - in the knowledge that red flags rarely become green. It is up to us therefore, to offer gentle but firm indication, of what jams harmoniously with our internal compass - and what very definitely jars!

The average of 5

Since we are the average of the five people with whom we spend our most time, it makes sense to evaluate and review our relationships regularly. Who are we most drawn to and why?

Ask yourself, if you were to spontaneously host a dinner party, and had the choice of inviting any five guests from your current life - who would they be and why? Consider friends, family, partners, co-workers, mentors - What character traits do your chosen guests embody? To whom do you excitedly offer a seat? To whom do you feel obliged to offer a seat, but don't necessarily prefer?

Repeat this exercise - this time choosing five guests you don't know. Perhaps they are deceased? From the world of rock, pop, fashion, entrepreneurship, academia, literacy, sport, spirituality? Again, ask yourself who would these guests be, and why?

This exercise informs a wealth of knowledge regarding our current relationships, as well as shedding light on the qualities we least and most admire – as well as those to which we secretly aspire! Remember, we become most like the people with whom we surround ourselves - so it makes sense to review our relationships regularly and honestly.

Final Word

Life isn't a dress rehearsal, so love the people who love you back. Enjoy the fun, the moments and the memories, and remember to pay less attention to the begrudgers, critics, haters and naysayers – they're usually confused fans!

> *"Think where man's glory begins and ends, and*
> *say, my glory was I had such friends."*
> *– W.B. Yeats*

6

LET'S TALK ABOUT SEX

Attraction

Have you ever had the experience of being literally stopped in your tracks by someone? I certainly have! Rendered speechless, in a heady rush, unintelligible, temporarily immobile - it's probably not my winning look! As the front seat passenger of an ex-boyfriend's car, I've also hilariously witnessed the powerful, automatic and transfixing effect of dopamine lighting up the male brain – resulting in a rear ended car in front! Luckily for him I had to pick myself up from laughing, knowing only too well the literal car crash effects of when our brains are lustfully hijacked!

Chemistry and Physiology

When we find people attractive, our limbic system or emotional brain becomes fired up, whilst our thinking brain, the prefrontal cortex, is rendered temporarily inactive - or appears so at least! Like hunger and thirst, sex is a basic physiological need, and consequently almost impossible to stamp out. It derives from the reptilian core of the brain - below the level of emotion or cognition. This primal area of the brain; associated with survival, focus, wanting, craving and motivation, is similarly activated when feeling a rush of cocaine (Fisher, 2004).

Dopamine is the neurotransmitter associated with motivation, possessing a healthy sex drive, and feeling sexy (Amen, 2009). Serotonin is similarly associated with a rush of positive emotion post orgasm, and since these feelings - post sex, are attributed largely to the release of these chemicals, we can see why for so many reasons sex is powerful, motivating and in certain cases, addictive. Dopamine is the ultimate pleasure centre - associated with wanting, caving and addiction. Norepinephrine, another chemical released during sexual activity - is associated with obsession or an inability to think about anything other than the other person with whom we're sexually active. Serotonin brings about the warm, fuzzy, "I'm in love" romantic feelings, and oxytocin - which is a by-product of the serotonin release, is responsible for our drive to bond with the other person (Maloof, 2022). With this cocktail chemical mix, it's perhaps easier to understand the concept of 'Crazy in Love' - cue Romeo and Juliet, Bonnie and Clyde, Marianne and Connell.....

"People pine for love, they live for love, they kill for love, they write poetry and songs for love, they die for love." (Fischer, 2004).

Sex, love and relationships are wonderful, yet complex. They are a potent combination of biology, chemistry, compatibility, connectivity, environment, climate, culture and preference. As with baking a great cake - having the right blend of ingredients largely determines the success and ultimate sauciness of the mix! Our childhood, cultural background, family, education and expectations similarly influence the people we find most attractive, and with whom we share most in common.

Author and Anthropologist, Dr. Helen Fisher, has completed extensive research on the evolution, expression and science of love, and states the impact of our biology, personality and environment in her bestselling books on the nature and chemistry of romantic love. Dr. Fisher purports we have evolved four very broad styles of thinking and behaviour as humans - which largely impact our chemistry and compatibility with others. She proposes that our thinking and behaviour styles are therefore heavily impacted by the following chemical messenger systems (Fischer, 2004):

1) Dopamine
2) Serotonin
3) Testosterone
4) Oestrogen

Whilst we are each a combination of all of the above neurotransmitters/chemical messenger systems, Dr. Fisher believes we generally dominate in one:

Personality Chemicals

Someone who is high in their Dopamine chemical expression will present as curious, creative, spontaneous, impulsive, energetic and mentally flexible. Conversely, someone with a high Serotonin expression will be more traditional, modest, conventional, apologetic, detail oriented and have a desire to follow rules. When these two meet and fall in love, their relationship may be very complementary in the early stages - the high dopamine person is grounded by the high serotonin individual, and the high serotonin person fires off the energy, creativity and adventure of the high dopamine individual. Cracks may appear however, if over time, the high dopamine person still yearns for thrills and adventure and wants to go backpacking through South East Asia for example, whilst the serotonin individual feels the responsibility of having two kids and a mortgage.

This may be similarly the case for someone with a high testosterone expression - pairing with someone who is more oestrogen dominant. The high testosterone individual will present as logical, analytical, tough-minded, decisive and direct; whilst the individual with a high oestrogen expression will be more sensitive, emotional and empathetic. Whilst the coupling of these two, may have the initial opposites attract magnetism - later in the relationship, the very qualities that once attracted them, may become a source of contention. What was previously seen as strong and powerful may be later perceived as ruthless and uncaring - and what was initially perceived as sensitive and kind, may be later seen as weak and over-emotional.

Communicating Effectively

Dr. Fischer purports that in relationships where individuals' dominant neurotransmitter system are different - each person must understand and communicate in the language their partner_understands (Fischer, 2014). For example, someone who is high in testosterone expression - therefore logical, goal-oriented and decisive, will be better communicated to in a clear, direct, concise manner, as opposed to appealing to their soft, romantic side (as it's harder for the person to access this system). Conversely, someone high in oestrogen expression - therefore empathetic and emotional, will be better communicated to with engagement, sensitivity, understanding, and a few love poems thrown in for good measure!

It's important to note that we each possess all four neurotransmitter chemical messenger systems - however to varying degrees, and with dominance generally leaning toward one of the four systems. It follows that the more familiar we are with our mate's dominant system, the more effective we will be in our communications with one another. (Fischer, 2014)

'The 5 Love Languages'

In his best-selling book, 'The 5 Love Languages', Author, Gary Chapman, proposes five ways for romantic partners to express and experience love (Chapman, 2015). They are as follows:

1) **Words of Affirmation**
2) **Quality Time**
3) **Receiving Gifts**

#DrDee

4) Physical Touch
5) Acts of Service.

Chapman suggests that each person has one primary and one secondary love language, and that in order to discover someone's love language, we might consider the following:

1) Observe how our partner most often expresses love to others
2) Note what they most often request
3) Note what they most often complain about

People tend to naturally give love in the way they like to receive it, and better communication may be facilitated between couples when each person demonstrates affection in the love language their partner prefers, and best responds.

For example, If one person's primary love language is **Physical Touch** - they are less likely to feel loved, appreciated or attracted by their partner doing laundry and household chores (Acts of Service) – unless of course their partner happens to be doing this in costume! For this person, physical touch is their primary love language - whether in the form of a full body massage or some other physical intimacy or physical connection.

For someone who's primary love language is **Acts of Service** - they will feel a greater sense of love and appreciation for their partner bringing out the rubbish or occupying the children for a few hours (Acts of service) instead of being sent a dozen red roses - **Receiving Gifts**.

The individual who's primary love language is **Words of Affirmation**, will get an immediate spike in dopamine on hearing words of praise, positivity and encouragement. They love to be validated by their partner through positive, supportive language, so the key to their heart is through affirmative words.

Quality Time is the love language cherished by individuals who value togetherness and undivided attention. They enjoy alone time with their partner, without the distraction of phones or other external demands.

According to Chapman, identifying, labelling, communicating and mastering each other's love language, will not only foster clear communication and understanding in romantic relationships - but will significantly enhance intimate relations overall (Chapman, 2015).

Basic, fundamental need

Sex is often perceived as an integral part of romantic relationships, with its presence or absence largely conjuring, denoting, defining and categorising the relationship - whether casual hook up, long term committed, friends with benefits, occasional dalliance or it's complicated! Psychologist, Abraham Maslow, in 1943, identified sex as one of the basic human needs, along with food, water and sleep - and whilst it may indeed be a basic physiological need, the emotional and psychological complexity of sex are anything but! Sex complicates everything! Not having sex complicates everything! No other human connection or disconnection makes us question - not only our relationship with another human, but our relationship with ourselves, and no other human act facilitates the physical proximity, emotional closeness, or nirvana state, most often associated with sex.

To some extent, we've been brainwashed by a soft-porn, hyper-sexualised society, which celebrates the aesthetics, performance and frequency of sex - resulting in many feeling defective if they fall short in any of these areas. But who's calling the standards? Most of us will agree that sexual desire and satisfaction are influenced by so much more than good timing, technique, performance and physicality? Sexual pleasure is more likely to be the combined effect of everything - not least of all our psychology and emotions, which impact our ability to truly synchronise and connect with someone in the bedroom – or elsewhere! Is the focus of attention therefore, not more accurately placed on the quality of our sexual expression and experience?

For example, if we're holding resentment of some description toward our partner, it's unlikely the earth will shatter for us sexually. The exception being perhaps where resentment is channelled into sexual passion – however, even this can leave an aftermath of emptiness and unresolved emotion. Sexual expression is therefore generally enhanced by open, shared communication, and by fully inhabiting our present state – mind, body, spirit and soul.

Turning our Attention Inward

Iconic Couples' Therapist and Author, Esther Perel, describes relationships today as being worlds apart from the simple, economic institutions of the past. Today she believes, we expect our partners to provide the anchoring experiences of security, safety and permanence - coupled with desire, unpredictability, playfulness, imagination and edge. We crave connection yet also need separation; we want intimacy yet also desire mystery; we want surprise yet we also need consistency. In short, we want the entire smorgasbord - and if it's not freely available, we question our compatibility.

"A crisis of desire however, is oftentimes simply a crisis of imagination". (Perel, 2019). We blame the other person for no longer turning us on, but do we turn ourselves on? Perel suggests our attention needs to be turned inward in the first instance, with regard to what makes us feel our best. What do we need to do or change in order to fill our own cup instead of blaming, complaining and trying to change or fix our partner? What makes us feel replenished, loved, desired, fulfilled, happy, joyful, sexy? What do we need to change or modify in our own lives to embody these feelings?

Generally, we are most connected and at ease with ourselves and our bodies, when feeling rested, fit, healthy, attractive, vital, energised, confident, valued in our relationships and fulfilled in our work. It also helps when we occupy the belief that we are making an important contribution to society and that we feel connected to our life's purpose (Perel, 2019). Anything we believe we're good at and enjoy doing, raises our energy vibration as well as our feelings of optimism, wellbeing and prosperity. This in turn results in a mirrored effect on every person and situation we come into contact - not least of all our sexual partners.

#DrDee

It makes sense therefore, that in order to bring the best to our relationships, we must first invest in ourselves. The better we feel, the greater our ability to receive and give pleasure. Most successful partnerships embrace and enjoy spending time apart – as they recognise that by independently investing and bringing something back of themselves, they contribute more effectively to the relationship as a whole (Perel, 2019). Thus by recognising and activating our passions, skills, talents and abilities, we release the potential to feel independently energised and supported by our wider interests, which in turn reflects in the attitude and playfulness we bring to our relationships.

Online Dating

Today, meeting online has become the norm in establishing romantic connections. With the click of a button, we gain immediate access to an array of potential suitors - for anything from casual hook-up to something a little more serious, and everything in-between! Online dating has eclipsed real life spontaneous encounters, yet there's never been as many people reporting feeling disillusioned by the online dating experience. We crave connection, attention, conversation, fun - yet the experience of endless texting back and forth can often have the opposite effect of leaving us feeling empty and disconnected. There's the additional factor of people not always matching their profile when a meeting occurs in reality, and then there's the inevitable question of chemistry, excitement and sparkle...

Online Dating is like a walk in the park – Jurassic Park! For the most part it's fun. It keeps us polished and on our dating toes, and like any skill - we get better with practice. We don't meet people by FedEx or DPD delivery. They don't just magically appear at our doors by sitting, scrolling, matching, liking, messaging and gathering online pen-pals! We need to put solid, robust action steps behind our intentions, and be as proactive in our dating practice as we are with everything else.

I've had my share of online dating experiences, most of which were great - well, with the exception of one or two (maybe for the next book!).

I chose two dating sites - each at different stages, so whilst I'm by no means a pro, one thing apparent is that there are loads of men - loads! and I suspect this is the case for whatever your mating preference happens to be. If you're brave enough to put yourself out there, put a bit of thought into your profile, express your genuine opinions and interests, and chat naturally - you'll stand out from the crowd. It's probably a good idea not to waste too much time either texting back and forth - you'll know more about someone from a brief phone call, or within the first five minutes of meeting in-person, than endless messaging back and forth.

If you're reading this and thinking about giving online dating a go, although a six pack might get you noticed – ease, sense of humour, originality, authenticity, and knowing the difference between 'your' and 'you're' win the race every time! In the words of Oscar Wilde, "Be yourself, everyone else is already taken."

Dating Tips

In her funny, yet practical book, 'How to Not Die Alone', Dating Coach and Hinge Relationship Scientist, Logan Ury, identifies 3 dating tendencies. These are ways of thinking or patterns of behaviour which interfere with people's ability to successfully find love.

1) The Romanticiser: This is the person who loves to love. They believe in a single, perfect soulmate occupying the single perfect relationship. This of course is a fallacy, since even the best relationships are imperfect and require consistent effort and attention.

2) The Maximiser: This is the person who holds the belief that no matter who they are with, they could do better. They remain in constant search of the next best thing, which evidently limits their capacity to sufficiently invest in or give their best to any one person.

3) The Hesitator: This is the person who postpones their love life based on feelings of inadequacy or limitation, e.g. "I'll go back

out dating as soon as I look better" or "As soon as I'm working again, I'll feel more confident about dating again."

Which one are you?

I've possibly been guilty of all three at different stages! I've also been heavily invested in the "spark" – if I didn't feel that initial pang of chemistry, it deterred me from considering a follow-up date. But perhaps a slow burner has more to offer than we think? Although honest, dependable and reliable are characteristics that occasionally get a bad wrap – a drama free relationship surely has its merits? Ultimately, we have to figure out what floats our boat and what our deal-breakers are. What characteristics and values would we like our date to embody? And do we ourselves match and embody such characteristics? Since who we are is ultimately who and what we attract, this becomes our road map to attracting someone with similarly aligned qualities, values and preferences.

Fanning the flames of Long Term Passion

When it comes to long term relationships, whilst the flames of passion and desire are very often present in the early stages, most couples report to this changing over time. For many, this results in the classic elephant in the room - where both parties are aware that things have changed on a sexual or intimate level, but neither is prepared to address the subject. This may lead to longer term negative implications for the relationship, so it's important to fan and renew the flames of passion - through shared communication, sustained effort, as well as maintaining an element of mystery and surprise.

American Sex Therapist, Dr. Cheryl Fraser, proposes that couples interested in cultivating and maintaining passion in their relationships work on three key elements (Fraser, 2019):

1)   Intimacy - Friendship

2) Thrill - Novelty/Erotic attraction
3) Sensuality - relating to one's significant other through the five senses: touch, taste, smell, hearing and seeing.

Dr. Fraser suggests that a truly satisfying relationship rarely happens by accident, and strong couples have a healthy balance of all three elements. She proposes taking planned, purposeful action, and letting go of the idea that the best sex involves spontaneous swinging from the chandeliers - instead agreeing a suitable time and place to be sexually intimate. Upon initial reading, this may seem jarringly business like, but consider the endless creative possibilities that could ensue in the waiting period - the sparkle of anticipation...

Mindful Communication

The first three minutes supposedly predict the outcome of any discussion to an 80% level (Fraser, 2019) so being conscious of our tone and demeanour makes approaching sensitive conversations easier. Masterful couples take responsibility for everything in their relationship - both individually and together, assuming the mind-set that both parties are in the relationship together and therefore are both invested in a positive outcome. Even where one person is clearly more responsible for a mistake or misdemeanour than the other, both are equally motivated to acknowledge, repair, and resolve to do better. Dr. Fraser suggests creating loving intentions together each morning, e.g. "I intend to be mindful of my tone of voice and not be impatient or snappy with you today" or "I commit to taking the children out for a few hours to give you a break" and so forth.

Perception v Reality

Everything is subjective and things generally only become problematic if and when we categorise, blame, or ascribe derogatory meaning to something. For example, a concern that frequently arises for couples is the frequency or intensity of their sex lives. Whilst the absence of affection, attention, intimacy and sexual connection may make people question among other things, their identity, virility, sexiness and worth - things may be further exacerbated by unhelpful labelling and comparisons. Netflix, social media, movies and porn are among the many culprits responsible for presenting an often contrived, filtered, curated and unrealistic representation of sex and relationships - and this can largely impact people's thinking styles, perceptions, performance and beliefs around same.

"Comparison is the thief of joy" – Eleanor Roosevelt

So often, we become consumed with how we measure up by comparison with other people. Should we be having more sex? Should our sex lives be hotter? Is it wrong to fantasise or self pleasure whilst in a relationship? Can relationships ever recover from infidelity? Does movie sex really exist? Is porn ever acceptable? What about fetishes and sex toys? What is tantric sex and who has time for it anyway? Are we still on the same page about monogamy? Is it ok to have coffee with an ex? How about sliding into someone's private/direct messages? Are we both on the same page about liking other people's pictures on social media?

The answers to these questions are as individual as the people asking - and may change over time. Communication in relationships is therefore key. Rather than comparing our situation to that of others - the focus of attention is better directed toward what feels right and in accordance with our particular set of standards, values, beliefs and desires at each life-stage. Take the time to communicate, ask questions, and remain as open and honest in one's sex life as everything else. By normalising and introducing supposedly taboo topics of conversation, we are paving the way for a more open and honest conversation to take place - both in and outside of relationships.

"I do....or maybe I don't?"

To date, I've had two opportunities to marry - neither of which I accepted. I learned however, that discussing this didn't always bode well. Despite living in a supposedly modern age, people's ideas and opinions can be quite antiquated when it comes to relationships and the institution of marriage. This references what I spoke of previously regarding belief systems and values. What we've been brought up to believe as categorical, undisputed truth, is surely something we are equipped to question and make a call on as adults?

If we differ in our perspective, that doesn't make anyone better or worse than the next - it simply makes us human. So without necessarily having to agree with another - by respectfully considering and holding space for differing perspectives, we broaden our mind-set and this facilitates more open and progressive dialogues to take place. It's also worth considering that at any stage, people can change their mind about anything - so it serves us to ponder things in less absolute, more fluid terms.

Relationship Diversity

Despite a wealth of research showing that being sexually active contributes to wellbeing and happiness (Muise et al, 2016), what about the people who drift into sexless relationships yet report being content? Or those who decide mutually to not have sex? Or those who for whatever reason can't have sex? What about those who choose to remain single and celibate, or single and dating? Those who swing or prefer polyamory? The defining word here is choice. Provided no one is being hurt, harmed, harassed or coerced – we are not obliged to add anything to our daily flossing and five a day, to comply with societal norms and standards of sexual convention. Rather, it is each person's choice, to decide what feels right and in accordance with their particular needs and preferences.

Relationships are therefore not a "one size fits all". There is no one way to have a relationship and there is no one way to sexually express. People often think of the term diversity in the context of gender and

#DrDee

ethnicity, however diversity is applicable to any subject – not least of all relationships and sex. Perhaps a scale or spectrum might be useful therefore, instead of norms and polarisations when considering contemporary relationship styles. Different styles and presentations work for different people, and thus, we are not positioned to claim moral superiority over others' preferences. As long as relations are fully-consensual, non-abusive and non-coercive, everyone deserves the right and freedom to choose.

Final musings

American Sexuality expert, Dr. Emily Morse, finishes her refreshingly honest, modern-day podcast, 'Sex with Emily', by asking her guests the following:

1) What is your biggest turn on?
2) What is your biggest turn off?
3) What for you makes good sex?
4) What is something you would tell your younger self in relation to sex and relationships?
5) What is the number one thing you wish everyone knew about sex?

"It's not true that I had nothing on. I had the radio on."
- Marilyn Monroe

#DrDee

ATTACHMENT STYLES IN ADULT RELATIONSHIPS

Introduction to Attachment

Authors, Levine & Heller, in their popular book, 'Attached', offer a succinct, modern take on relationships, and how adults' behaviour in romantic relationships are influenced by the three main attachment styles: Secure, Anxious and Avoidant, These three attachment styles were initially identified by Developmental Psychologists, Mary Ainsworth in the 1970s, who expanded upon John Bowlby's initial attachment research in the 1950s and 60s. Bowlby was interested in understanding the distress that children experience when separated from their primary caregivers, and found that attachment was characterised by clear behavioural and motivation patterns. When children are frightened, they seek proximity from their primary caregiver in order to receive both comfort and care. Bowlby & Ainsworth's ground breaking research on Attachment Theory highlighted the importance of the bond between parent and child in fostering a strong relationship connection, or a failure to thrive. Their studies showed that connection between the infant and caregiver was as essential to the child as basic food and water, and resulted in the infant developing a particular attachment style throughout their lives – Secure, Anxious or Avoidant

Anxious, Avoidant & Securely Attached

Throughout history, children who maintain proximity to an attachment figure are more likely to receive comfort and protection, and are therefore more likely to survive to adulthood (Cherry, 2022). The following offers some helpful summary points taken from the recent work of Levine & Heller, regarding the impact of attachment styles on adult relationships. Whether you have just started dating someone or have been married for thirty years, each of us fall into one of these three categories - or a combination of anxious and avoidant (Levine & Heller (2019).

- **Secure Attachment:** Secure people generally feel comfortable with intimacy. They expect their partners to be warm, loving and responsive, and don't worry much about losing their partner's love.
- **Anxious Attachment:** People with an anxious attachment style crave intimacy, have a tendency to feel inferior to their partner, and may become worried or preoccupied about their partner not reciprocating their love.
- **Avoidant Attachment:** People with avoidant attachment style equate intimacy with loss of autonomy and independence. They constantly try to minimise closeness, through deactivating strategies such as distancing, withholding emotion and keeping secrets.

As humans, we each have a basic need to form close bonds – however, the way we create these bonds differs. Someone with an avoidant attachment style might wager it less prudent to invest their time and energy into becoming attached to just one person - since he/she/they may not be around for very long. On the opposite end, someone with an anxious attachment style is likely to display hypervigilance, conscientiousness and persistence about remaining close to their love interest. Someone with a secure attachment style responds assertively in relationships - communicating their needs and expectations in a gentle, but firm manner. This is not to label the avoidant or anxious attachment style as pathological - rather to examine each in the context of whether or not they effectively serve an individual in their adult relationships.

Protest Behaviours & Fight or Flight

Levine & Heller identify protest behaviours as going hand in hand with anxious attachment styles. Protest behaviours are essentially primitive behavioural representations of a strong emotional reaction. This explains why a child parted from his/her/ their parent becomes frantic - crying uncontrollably until contact is re-established with the parent or attachment figure.

Protest behaviours may also be similarly present in adult relationships. If someone is on a night out and forgets to message their partner who happens to have an anxious attachment style - this may provoke protest behaviour. In an escalating state of worry, the anxious individual's pre frontal cortex, i.e. thinking, insightful part of the brain becomes hijacked by the limbic/emotional brain - which leads to a flood of irrational thoughts and impulsive behaviours, e.g. sending frantic texts, leaving several voice messages, storming out etc. This is due to the anxious person's inability to address their irrational thoughts and appropriately calm their nervous systems.

Once aware of this tendency to enter the fight or flight response quickly, the person with an anxious attachment style can learn the skills of how to independently moderate and calm their nervous system. This may be done through a variety of techniques such as breathing, grounding and relaxation exercises, mindfulness, meditation, cognitive behaviour therapy and engaging in better thought hygiene and management. Partners of individuals' with an anxious attachment style also play a role in minimising the fears and anxieties of their anxious partners once these have been identified.

Avoidant Attachment Style

People with an avoidant attachment style use deactivating strategies to keep themselves at arm's length from their partner. Such strategies may include not calling for several days after an intimate date, forming relationships with unavailable people - or with people with whom there is little possibility of a future. They may also keep secrets or leave things vague to maintain a feeling of independence or emotional distance. People with this avoidant style may also avoid physical closeness, or flirt with others to provoke insecurity in their relationship. They may additionally focus on their partner's minor imperfections. (Levine & Heller, 2019)

Although avoidant individuals are shown to have a great deal of self-confidence about not needing anyone - their self-belief comes with a price tag. This is demonstrated through studies, where individuals with avoidant attachment style scored lowest on every measure of closeness in personal relationships - being less willing to self-disclose, engage in intimacy, or seek help from others (Couelle, 2014). Along with a self-reliant attitude, someone with avoidant attachment style can train themselves to not care how the person closest to them is feeling, and this lack of empathy results in their partners often complaining about not receiving sufficient emotional support. It also leads to lack of connectedness, warmth and overall satisfaction in their wider relationships. (Levine & Heller, 2019)

Seeking Support for Avoidant Attachment Style

With an awareness of how their close relationships are adversely impacted, the avoidant individual may seek support in learning the skills to develop better personal awareness and communication strategies around their distancing actions. Whilst acknowledging their need for space - whether emotional and/or physical, the avoidant individual may learn to better communicate this in a sensitive manner. For example, an individual with an avoidant attachment style may respectfully explain their need for time out or time alone - adding reassurance that this is not a problem with their partner, but rather their own personal need for space in any relationship. Their partner is then less likely to become offended or to intensify their efforts of drawing closer to the avoidant individual - allowing them to make an informed decision about whether or not the relationship meets their expectations of intimacy.

Anxious and Avoidant Pairing

Levine & Heller (2019) propose that there is a gravitational pull between anxious and avoidant individuals - such that when they become attached, it's difficult for them to let go. The reason people in an anxious-avoidant relationship find it difficult to move toward greater relationship security, is primarily because they are trapped in a cycle of triggering and exacerbating each other's insecurities. People with an anxious attachment style cope with threats to their relationship by activating their attachment systems - clinging and trying to get closer to their partner, whilst people who are avoidant employ more deactivating strategies to create distance. The closer the anxious individual tries to get, the more distant the avoidant becomes. In order to overcome this unhelpful seesaw effect, both individuals need to firstly become aware of their attachment style and corresponding behavioural responses, and work toward both becoming more secure in their communication of these with one other.

5 Principles of Secure and Effective Communication (Levine & Heller, 2010)

1) Be emotionally brave. Effective communication requires being completely honest and genuine about one's feelings.
2) When communicating, focus on your needs and desires as opposed to labelling, judging or criticising your partner's shortcomings.
3) State precisely what is bothering you. Be specific and avoid any confusion from the outset.
4) Avoid blame and accusations. Never make your partner feel incompetent, inadequate or inherently bad. Separate and label the behaviour of concern - as opposed to labelling the person.
   Use "I" terms, for example, "I found your tone of voice aggressive when you said 'x' …It made me feel 'y'…." instead of "You're such an aggressive person, what did I ever see in you!"
5) Communicate your relationship needs calmly, assertively and without apology. Although your feelings may not be shared by

your partner, it is important they are heard and given due air time, acknowledgment, and respect.

The Dependency Paradox

Attachment principles teach us that most people are only as needy as their unmet needs. When individuals' emotional needs are met, they usually turn their attention outward to matters external to themselves. This is sometimes referred to in the attachment literature as the "dependency paradox" (Levy, 2021) - meaning the more healthily people look toward each other for support, the more independent and daring they become in their outward lives. This explains how individuals in satisfying relationships are often seen to blossom - both internally and externally.

Yet paradoxically, we live in a culture that celebrates self-reliance, independence and bullet-proof self-confidence and boundaries - frequently minimising the softer characteristics of closeness, intimacy, trust, vulnerability and interdependency. The prevailing notion is that too much dependence in adult relationships is a bad thing. However, the fact remains that the need for intimate connection and the reassurance and support of others plays a vital role for humans throughout their lives, from infancy to adulthood (Bowlby, 1997).

Secure Communication Strategies

Adult attachment theory has proved time and again that when it comes to attachment style, nothing is written in stone and it's never too late to re-write and learn new and better relationship and communication skills (Levine & Heller, 2019). The key point is having the willingness and desire to recognise, acknowledge, and overcome our own default patterns in the first instance. With such increased self-awareness, we are then better placed to understand and be more open and supportive in our relationships - with less primitive communication and reaction styles. Thus, instead of attempting to impose what we desire on another, we are more

#DrDee

likely to calmly assert our preference and decide respectfully, whether or not the relationship is worth our continued investment.

"The propensity to make strong emotional bonds to particular individuals is a basic component of human nature."
– John Bowlby

#DrDee

THE PSYCHOLOGY
OF FASHION

Sign of the Times

Historically, fashion and clothes have offered a potent visual of the cultural and socio-economic landscape. Few places, other than the streets, better represent social, political or cultural change. During World Wars I and II, clothes were made as practical and cost-efficient as possible. The 1930's Great Depression observed low-key conservatism replacing the flamboyant flapper style of the 1920's. The 50's brought about a revival of the cinched waist and combed-back hair, whilst the 60's micro-mini and rebellious prints reflected the civil rights movement and anti-war protests. Hippie vibes punctuated the 1970s and the 80s were all about punk, neon and big hair. The 90s brought about boot-cut flares and camis, and the noughties - as described by Rindfuss (2009), are a global mash-up of it all.

In troubled times, pared back lines often characterise the mood du jour – the exception being the 1960s, where fashion became a rebellious backlash of the times. But what of this new era? March 2020 marked the beginning of the Covid-19 global pandemic, where clothes pretty much became an extension of people's homes. Sharp structure and corporate

PSYCHOLOGY WITH A SPARKLE

edginess were replaced with comfort, softness and ease - a direct contrast to the turbulent external backdrop of fear and uncertainty. Survival ruled the day - as cosy, sustainable loungewear, cushioned the sharp blow to our physical, social, emotional and economic landscape. Among others, style elevation details took a back-seat, as people nestled, reflected, introspected and re-evaluated what was individually and collectively most important.

The Psychology of Clothes

Clothes short-circuit the necessity to convey something verbally. Whether consciously or otherwise, what we wear tells a story. It can be an effective way of channelling a message - to ourselves and to others. When we look good on the outside, the implication is generally that we feel more confident on the inside – which isn't always the case. Clothes may be used as a camouflage - to distract from challenging of difficult life circumstances, and when feeling poorly within. Whatever the case, our choice of clothing conveys important non-verbal cues regarding our internal and external states, and since confidence is about the best outfit anyone can rock – our sartorial presentation can influence how we relate to others on a social and interactive level.

Whilst researching material for this chapter, I came across an interview with Singer and Composer, Sir Elton John, who expressed the importance of getting into costume and treating each of his shows as an occasion: "It was part of the ritual of performing - I couldn't wear jeans because I was too fat for jeans, but I had to get into costume - where there was an element of theatre, drama, occasion, performance." This description accurately captures the psychology underpinning clothes and fashion. Clothes offer an instant snapshot to the world regarding our perceived state – physically, mentally, psychologically and emotionally. They enable us to portray and highlight certain aspects of our character and personality, whilst minimising others - and although we're not all performing on the world stage as in the case of Elton John (although Shakespeare would disagree – "All the world is a stage, with the men and women merely players"), what we wear hugely impacts our individual and collective psychology.

Non-verbal Communication

Social Psychologist and Author, Amy Cuddy - in her famously viral Ted Talk, 'Your body language may shape who you are', describes how body language shapes who we are as individuals. Cuddy describes how we make inferences and judgments about others from body language and non-verbal communication. By making slight tweaks or changes to our posture and how we communicate non-verbally, this can affect not only our thoughts, emotions and physiology - but also, it predicts real life outcomes regarding how we are received by others (Cuddy, 2012).

Clothes are a form of non-verbal communication which can either el-evate, neutralise, or weaken our delivery and performance. Our carriage generally changes - to reflect a more up-right posture when we're well-dressed, and we're more inclined to lean toward people than away. Fashion can thus enhance or subdue an entrance; improve or inhibit a performance, and complement or dilute a pitch. In the words of Celebrity Stylist Rachel Zoe - "Clothes are a way of saying who we are, without having to speak."

Mark of respect

Clothes often represent the stature of an occasion or person, e.g. a Movie Star on Oscar night, a Bride on their wedding day, the Pope in his papal robes. With each defining reference, we can immediately conjure an image of the person - visualising with remarkable precision, the colour, texture and overall appearance of the occasion. Style and detailing there-fore, not only offer an outward impression of a person, they also create an inner essence or sense of the person - giving life to Marc Jacobs' quote, "Clothes mean nothing until someone lives in them."

Dating back to biblical times, many references were made to the significance of garments and clothing. One of the first mentions of clothes as bearing important representation, was in the parable of the wedding feast in the New Testament (Matthew, 22:12). This tells of a man's attendance at a wedding, who wasn't wearing a wedding garment. The man was reportedly without an excuse for this, to which the King ordered that he be thrown out into the darkness. A bit harsh I would've thought – although the parable effectively illustrates reference to clothes bearing historic significance. Modern day international Fashion Designer, Tom Ford, echoes this sentiment in his suggestion, "You should put on the best version of yourself when you go out into the world, because it is a show of respect to the people around you".

Dressing well offers unmistakable benefits to mood, mind-set and confidence. Good grooming and a considered dress sense signals to the world that we take pride in ourselves and in our appearance - and equally that we value, honour and respect those with whom we share and extend company. Whatever our physique, it's possible to look well on any budget. We don't have to fork out hundreds on items we can't afford, rather if we develop the habit of shopping our own wardrobes - seeing what's appropriate to the occasion, it's possible to look and feel smart, as well as enhancing our confidence.

"Get up, Dress up and Show up for Life."
(unknown)

Depending on what's happening within and around us, our best may vary from time to time. Certain days, our best may be the simple act of successfully managing to get out of bed in the morning, whilst on others, we may be up for a full-on style challenge. Whatever the case, it's important we choose in a self-supporting manner - without judgment. As well as being our best currency, the energy we extend to others is our unique responsibility. We get to choose how colourfully we present each day – in a metaphorical as well as a physical sense. Do we shine or dull the atmosphere? Do we elevate or depress? Hinder or help? Illuminate or darken?

Whilst we can't bypass our emotions via clothes, styling and paraphernalia, there is an undisputed brightening effect on our unique and collective psychology, when we are effortful in our style and presentation. We feel better about ourselves when we are effortful in all areas of our lives – including our work, relationships, our family and personal lives, our friendships, and our physical appearance. By extension, the people around us are consciously and unconsciously affected by our physical and psychological energy also.

Clothes and colour therefore, have an inward and outward impact. In terms of colour suggestions - red is thought to convey confidence, passion and dominance (think of former presidents' ties). Purple infers opulence, regality, aristocracy (consider historic kings and queens). Orange conveys optimism and motivation; yellow radiates happiness and creativity; green is synonymous with abundance and renewal, whilst blue reflects calm and serenity.

Dark colours equally evoke their own poetic charm. Consider the magical properties of black and slate grey, which exude an air of depth, mystery, knowledge, coolness, intrigue….

The 'X' Factor

Whether or not we opt for bright colours, or choose to take a walk on the dark side - the style or X- factor most often emanates from within. It's that inner essence – the "je ne sais quoi"; which is most often complimented by clothes, but never eclipsed by them. Clothes and accessories therefore enhance the person's external appearance, but rarely short-circuit what needs to be emotionally addressed within. It follows, that if we rock up somewhere with a great suit and a bad attitude – it's not our suit that will be most remembered, but the attitude.

How we invest in ourselves inwardly therefore, is what gets reflected and projected outward – clothes and appearance therefore, are merely the final, superficial layer. If we're putting good stuff in, the likelihood is, that what comes out will be good also. This idea is beautifully captured in the words of Novelist, Roald Dahl, "If you have good thoughts, they will shine out of your face like sunbeams, and you will always look lovely."

Why bother?

The Covid-19 pandemic greatly impeded people's mood, buoyancy and general motivation to complete even the smallest, most routine task. Our lives were suddenly and drastically uprooted - which for many resulted in an inability to brush their teeth in the morning – let alone putting thought into what to wear! With so many real life worries happening globally, surely what we wore was the least of anyone's concern?

Without doubt, the pandemic inspired many to re-examine and re-evaluate their values and priorities – which resulted in positive knock-on effects for many. With such background turbulence and uncertainty, clothes and fashion became almost blasphemous to even consider as occupying any real importance or function - other than durable sustainability. For others however, shopping became an addiction – a way of coping with restricted life choices and the removal of civil liberties. Along with porn, alcohol, excess food, gambling and drugs, online shopping filled the void that had been previously filled by external and other pursuits.

Identity and Appearance

As humans, we often construct narratives around our perceived identity, which very often include how we present physically. For example, we may have the thought, "I've been hanging around in my pyjamas/boxers/dressing gown all day, I'm such a slob". Whilst there's nothing wrong with having the odd pyjama day, the thinking which may be generated from repeat episodes of same, may not be conducive to showing up at our best. Much depends on our mind-set, thought hygiene, and how robust we are in our psychology and identity. If we view or equate not getting dressed with being a "slob", or being a lazy or bad person - that's the story we will tell ourselves - and by default, that is how we will show up in the world.

Persistent critical self talk feeds a negative self-image, which leads to feelings of diminished self-confidence, and low self-worth. This impacts how we relate to ourselves firstly, and to the people in our close and extended networks. Hence, this is why it's so important to listen to the internal voice of higher consciousness as it pertains to all aspects of our daily choices and decision making – including how we physically show-up. If we can happily let ourselves off the hook every now and again, and we're cool with having the odd lounge day - that's wonderful. However, if out of habit or disinterest this becomes a regular occurrence, it may indicate a deeper internal struggle - best discussed with a trusted friend or professional.

Judging by Appearances

When we fail to invest time and energy into ourselves, there is a greater chance of our being critical and resentful toward others. Thus, if we know deep down we are violating a personal standard by not acting in way which is in accordance with the personal standards and values we have set for ourselves - we are more likely to harshly judge ourselves and others. Those who are acting as a mirror to our unmet personal standard, become the source of our jealousy and insecurity projections. For example, if we've been dragging ourselves around for days, unkempt, hopping from one Netflix show to the next, eating rubbish, not exercising - and some buff dude or glamorous gazelle pops up on our Instagram feed #livingtheirbestlife (supposedly), this may evoke a reaction!

Instead of allowing judgment, criticism and the green eyed monster take hold, a better response is to become curious about our reaction. If we scratch below the initial primitive surface reaction of jealousy or judgment - what are the underlying emotions trying to communicate? Important messages come to us through observing our reactions to others (positive and negative). Therefore, instead of allowing ourselves to remain stuck in the anger/resentment/jealousy or whatever the case is – if we instead reflect on what the emotion is here to teach, we learn and evolve exponentially.

Are we being presented with an image or real life situation, to inspire better self-care? Are we being triggered by someone to get healthier? Fitter? To seek support? To establish a better daily routine? To pursue healthier choices? Remember, the person or situation onto whom the reaction is being projected, is a messenger and potential catalyst for personal growth and change. They are merely a mirror being held to our own face -reflecting back where an action step is required. Be grateful for this unconscious prompt, and channel this energy into creating something proactive, nurturing and positive - instead of allowing bitterness, resentment and anger take hold.

Fashion and Style Influence

In the same way as our choices, interests, desires and reactions reveal aspects of our personality - what we wear gives immediate insight to our unique fingerprint expression also. Fashion choices offer instant communication to the world regarding our suggested confidence, sexuality, sensuality, creativity, worldliness, influence, individuality, character and signature style. It is a form of instant communication - a creative means of expression through personally chosen clothes, details and architecture. Personal style extends beyond material threads however, infusing our individual and collective psychology. Style is reflected in everything - from our clothes, to our homes, work, relationships, friendships, hobbies, interests, preferences and values.

Irish Poet and Playwright, Oscar Wilde, who lectured in Aesthetics, and was known for his satirical turn of phrase as well as sartorial flamboyance, quipped the following, "It is only shallow people who do not judge by appearances", whilst former Creative Director of Chanel, Karl Lagerfeld, suggested, "A respectable appearance is sufficient to make people more interested in your soul." Whilst both remarks share a similar irony, they also capture an inescapable truth - fashion is both an influencer and an influence, and we never do get a second chance to make a first impression! Since this is the case, perhaps it makes stylish as well as practical sense, to give some inward thought to our outward expression?

Psychology and Fashion

I've always been moved by the nature and influence of psychology in fashion, and just how much we can learn about people from how they dress. Fashion Designers mirror the cultural, psychological, political and socioeconomic climate in their aesthetic designs, whilst Psychologists to some degree, reflect the social, emotional and cognitive landscape. Both offer scaffolding - whether in the form of physical or emotional protection, and an adaptability in the interpretation of individual personality, character, expression and style.

If I hadn't become a Psychologist, I suspect I would have eventually ended up doing something in fashion or otherwise related. As a little girl, my career aspirations included becoming a Circus Performer (I may have achieved that to some extent!), an Actress, Popstar, and a Television Presenter. As my Mum recently expressed, "It was never anything ordinary for our Neesie". Like all children, I had big dreams and saw life in bold, playful, exuberant colour. However, similar to many households, such "unsteady" kinds of jobs were rarely encouraged - so when I'd raise the subject, it was immediately shot down in favour of something more "realistic" or "steady". Luckily for me, I have no regrets about where my career choices have taken me - I love my work as a Psychologist, although without doubt, I remain a dedicated follower of fashion!

> **"Let's do what we love and do a lot of it"**
> **– Marc Jacobs**

For those who love it, fashion evokes a fun, frivolous escape from the too-often seriousness of life – offering energetic impact, style and gravitas. Consider a vibrant lipstick for instant pucker; a brightly coloured tie for confidence and edge; a bespoke suit for something a little extra; a trilby hat for simple classic cool; a little black dress for understated sexy; the perfect fitting jeans when simply nothing else will do; a killer stiletto for statement glam; trainers for street style cool; a classic white shirt for instant freshness; a biker jacket for rock-star cool….

Whilst studying the creations of various Fashion Designers and street-style looks, we discover the quality, detail and style to which we're most uniquely drawn. What calls to us most loudly? (authentic self) What whispers in our ear? (aspiring self) What wishes we might give it a go? (courageous self) What insights absolute fear? (shadow self). Are we more attracted to bright, ornate patterns? Contemporary or vintage? Do we prefer a more tailored, bespoke feel to things? Subdued and under-stated, or loud and proud? Classical chic or rock- star cool? Whether it's virtual shopping, or real life trips - fashion affords endless opportunities for imagination, inspiration, interpretation and playful expression. As Jean-Luc Godard remarked, "It is not where you take things from, it is where you take them to."

Background Context and Style Inception

As a little girl, I loved nothing more than sitting on the edge of my parent's bed, and watching my Mum get ready to go out. She chose mod-esty over sexiness, old school glamour over grunge, bespoke over mass produced, and if ever I commented in relation to her clothes, makeup or jewellery, "Maybe put this on too? ", she would most often reply, "All you ever need is enough". My mother bought minimally, but well. She loved elegant, tailored designs in block colours, with unexpected trims. This followed through in 'most everything from her choice of home furnishings, to her silver and glass-wear; her signature jewellery pieces, classic leather bag, and never-leave-the-house perennial berry lip colour, "I couldn't go anywhere without my lipstick". Coming from a horse breeding background, perhaps she understood that as with race horses, Christmas decorations, poetry and responding to tricky emails - "Elegance is the art of good grooming and conscious restraint" (Sarah Ban Breathnach, 1997). Coco Chanel echoed this in her suggestion; "Before you leave the house, look in the mirror and take one thing off."

My father on the other hand, was a classic non- conformist - who special-ised in the art of extra. Charismatic and gregarious, he loved colouring outside the lines and rare stuck to the rules. As a child, I remember my Mum laying his clothes on the bed when they were going to a dance or function - in the hope she might inspire a little less crazy, more colour co-ordinated look. He was rarely compliant! He had his own particular style, which extended much beyond clothes. Whilst my mother favoured simple classics with a distinctive twist, my father was always on the co-lourful side. He had a bold, more eccentric style, which included bright colours, crazy ties, polka dot socks, tweed jackets, belted coats, bow ties for rugby matches, and a hat for every occasion!

My Mum recalls their first home where my Dad briefly lived prior to their being married. True to form, he reportedly painted the intersections of each stair-step with a different colour - which he clearly thought was charming, whilst my mother didn't quite share the same enthusiasm! In their second home, Daddy apparently painted one room in seven differ-ent colours prior to my Mum's arrival. Not quite sure how or where he managed to incorporate all seven, but needless to say they didn't remain for very long!

Platforms, Diamonds and Role Play

Dating back to childhood years, my love for all things girlie and glam were apparent – with distinct early Imelda Marcos tendencies! I have vivid memories as a 4/5 year old trotting around our home in my Mum's Abba-esque style white platforms – with which I was utterly obsessed. In my head, I was a Popstar or Actress, dramatically pushing a bright red pram - with two adorable little puppies inside (a black and a brown guy). Unfortunately, the top of the pram was slightly dodgy - so without a moment's notice, it would fly off unexpectedly, with the two little pups inside. I remember the brown guy being slightly slow on the uptake - which I now suspect was to do with him being tossed about in that dodgy red pram. Poor little guy was most likely in a permanent state of semi-concussion!

Makeup, perfume and jewellery were other firm favourites to which I regularly helped myself. My Mum recalls the story of when her engage-ment ring went missing, and searching the house "for three solid days". Frustrated, and beginning to give up hope of ever finding her precious gem again, suddenly she spotted a shining apparition in the laundry basket - "in one of your little socks"! Relieved beyond all, my Mum asked about this mystery retrieval - to which I reportedly went to great lengths to explain how, "I put it on that toe, and then I put it on that toe, and then ..." You get the gist – the ring was found, the world was put to rights, and all was forgiven. Evidently, I knew from an early age that the best place for diamonds, were on the soles of a girl's feet!

Primary school years demonstrated the early markers of an aspiring fashionista also. I would regularly change my hair and shoes at lunch-time – because, well, you know - it was important have a different look for the afternoons! My sister recalls the story of when we were taken to get winter wellingtons, and whilst she got "yellow wellies", I insisted on cream snow boots with a block heel......I mean seriously, the notions!

> **"But let's not forget, fashion is a game; getting dressed up is wanting to play."**
> **– Henri Lefebvre**

Sometimes by remembering who we were as children, helps us to recover and embrace fully who we are as adults. As children, we were fearless, curious, creative, confident - we played more and worried less. As adults, we sometimes lose the ability to be spontaneous and free, and by tapping into the wisdom and imagination of our childhood selves, we are given access to a wonderland of freedom and unselfconsciousness. Magical aspects of our personality are uncovered, as we discover a treasure trove of knowledge and insight about our hidden childhood selves. Who he/she/they were? How they played and what they loved? What might they do as adults? And how might we inject some of their style, sass and pizzazz into our everyday lives? (Sarah Ban Breathnach, 1997)

Adult Amateur Fashion Portfolio

Since my early 20s, I did my share of part-time modelling and photographic work. Pretty local stuff I might add - at 5ft 4, I was never exactly destined for the international runway, but I loved it and got a great kick out of trying out different looks and being part of various shoots, shows, promotions and events. Being a bit of a short-ass, the majority of the paid, professional work that came my way was either photographic or promotional, and always quite random – I'd meet someone on the social or fitness scene who was working in the fashion or photography industry, or I'd get talking to a professional who was in some way connected.

Although my experience of being connected to the fashion industry was very much a part-time hobby - as with everything, it offered some important take-home lessons, which can be applied to pretty much any life area. These included the value of head to toe grooming, styling, smiling, smizing (smiling with the eyes), posture, having a pleasant attitude, confident demeanour, skilled photographer and professional work ethic.

On the flip side, I learned how existing insecurities can become heightened in the world of exteriors and aesthetics, and how easily one can get caught up with comparisons, self-doubt, and an unhealthy fixation on surface attributes. What can I say? It only took a Doctorate in Psychology, a therapist, and the entire self-help section of the library to establish otherwise!

I jest! There were obviously other factors in my case, which were negatively impacting my confidence. I was lucky to be surrounded by genuinely sound people in the industry, and for the most part, we had many laughs and great fun.

The beauty and fashion industry are not for the faint-hearted however, and they require a robust mental and emotional framework – especially for anyone considering it on a more professional, full-time basis. Whilst it's wonderful to look and feel good on the outside, our greatest work begins on the inside, in cultivating a confident, healthy interior. Our personality and character therefore, how we think, the spirit and kindness we extend to others, our integrity and presence, the sparkle in our eye....they're the real style stars, which will see us through the many runways of life.

"Style is something each of us already has, we just need to find it."
– Diane von Furstenberg.

If something doesn't feel right, it most likely isn't. It makes practical as well as psychological sense therefore, to notice what feels immediately good when we try it on. Our initial instinct or reaction to what we wear is probably most reflective of our authentic style. If we're not 100% convinced at initial try-on stage, the chances are we'll be even less so with time. Therefore, it's probably a good idea, to only invest in pieces we absolutely adore. By delaying immediate gratification, we're more likely to find something special, which is truly reflective of our authentic character and style. As writer Jocasta Innes reminds us "Food for the eye is to be found almost everywhere". It takes discipline therefore, as well as a trained eye, to avoid spending money on items we don't truly need or that don't bring us joy – cue Marie Kondo, "Discard anything that does not spark joy."

Reflecting on my own purchasing history, some of my most beloved, interesting and sustainable pieces, were made abroad - mainly Italy, where I always feel more relaxed and at ease. I adore Italian fashion, and the entire Italian culture - including the people, the weather, the history, the architecture, food, art, vino, mediterranean vistas, the music, soul, the passion! Simply being in Italy (north or south) and relishing the experience, is for me as rewarding, as the shopping trips for sumptuous Italian leather and impeccable style. That's not to say I don't buy! However, I tend to buy better and well - choosing unique pieces that last the test of time, and remain perennially stylish.

"Fashions fade, style is eternal."
– Yves Saint Laurent

So what exactly is style? I believe style possesses an inner charm - which radiates beyond material threads. It's knowing that we don't necessarily need the most expensive watch, darkest tan, biggest diamond, shortest skirt, fastest car, biggest home, newest trainers, latest bag, or the largest social media following to stand out from the crowd. Style is inherent and possesses a self-reliant knowing of what feels and looks authentically good. Without being overly pushy or imposing, style has an understated confidence - which is often punctuated, though not exclusively accompanied by a distinct dress sense.

Like a fine wine, style is generally refined over time. As we begin to better-know ourselves, we trust our instinct regarding what works well and what doesn't. Style embodies an indefinable elegance therefore, which is felt as well as seen. It has a quiet, magnetising effect - causing a fascination with the wearer, as much as the clothes. Think of Grace Kelly, James Dean, Audrey Hepburn, Marilyn Monroe, Sean Connery, Princess Diana – timeless, graceful, elegant, chic; these legendary icons were 'influencers' and had something 'extra', before the terms were even popular or cool. We glimpse their old photos and see the person first, then what they are wearing - not the other way around.

> **In the words of French Fashion Designer, Christian Lacroix, "Elegance is not to pass unnoticed, but to get to the very soul of who one is."**

Fashion is no longer the elusive niche of historic aristocrats, movie stars, or Vogue and Vanity Fair readers. Fashion has very much earned its mainstream respected status - traversing all genders, platforms, and walks of life. This is perhaps no further evidenced, than in the sharp rise of Fashion Bloggers, Stylists and Image Consultants – many of whom, make a successful living from influencing people with styling and what to wear. Recent years have seen a greater leaning toward sustainable fashion – buying well and buying less. This encourages us to shun the allure of fast fashion, inciting a greater degree of consciousness on the impact of overconsumption, and how we individually and collectively play a role in protecting the environment.

Final Fashionable Note

Whatever your preference, fashion is expression. It is a means of creating, experimenting and having fun. There are no rules with fashion, so why not invent and enjoy your own? If you make a supposed 'fashion faux pas' (which I believe there's no such thing), don't worry! As long as you're feeling good, and love the skin you're in – you'll be impervious to the fashion critics in any event, and your sparkle will shine through......

Now that's true rockin' roll stye!

> *"The only real elegance is in the mind; if you've*
> *got that, the rest really comes from there"*
> *– Diana Vreeland, Former Editor in chief of Vogue*

9

SPIRITUALITY, LIFE, LOSS AND PURPOSE

Man's Search for Meaning

During one of the Covid-19 lockdowns, I was compelled to re-read Viktor Frankl's 1945 classic, 'Man's Search for Meaning'. This significant work offers Frankl's autobiographical proposal for coping in times of adversity. As a Viennese Psychiatrist, he survived years of unspeakable horror during World War II. His premise, "To live is to suffer, to survive, is to find meaning in the suffering", contemplated that man's primary motivation is to search for and find meaning in life. Frankl observed the way he and others coped during their time in Auschwitz Nazi concentration camps, noting that it was the men who comforted others - those who gave away their last piece of bread, who survived the longest.

Frankl's predecessor, Freud, had proposed a reductionist stance, that man's behaviour can be reduced to the conscious and unconscious pursuit of pleasure, whilst Nietzsche offered that man is driven by the will for power alone. Frankl advanced both perspectives, suggesting that people only settle for the pursuit of pleasure or power, when they fail to find meaning in their lives. Man's primary motivation therefore he believed, was to find meaning even in the midst of dire circumstances.

Choosing our Response

Playwright, William Shakespeare believed, "Nothing is either good or bad, but thinking makes it so." We get to choose each day, in each moment, how we think about and respond to life's situations, circumstances, people and events. It's easy to remain happy and optimistic when life positively flows and we get the breaks, but what about the times when we're compelled to deal with challenges, pain, struggle, suffering, loss and frustration? In these moments, we are called to confront ourselves on a much deeper level - observing who we are and what we're about when things don't go our way.

Do we blame, shame, criticise, complain, assume victimhood and divert personal responsibility? Do we spend days, months and years ruminating about how difficult life is, and how we've been dealt a raw hand, or how this person or that has wronged us in some way, which gives us entitlement to remain bitter, angry and resentful?

Or, do we attempt to get on with life as best and as pleasantly as we can - showing up for the good times and bad; doing the inner work required to acknowledge and process our childhood traumas, and taking personal responsibility for our lives and happiness?

> **"The greatest difficulty is the mental resistance to things that arise, and the underlying assumption that they somehow should not."**
> **- Eckhart Tolle.**

Our automatic response to most challenge and suffering is, "Why me?" "Why is this happening to me?" "I'm a good person, I don't deserve this." Sadly no one is exempt from human suffering, and if we can somehow train our minds to ask the question instead, "Why not me?" or "What is this here to teach me?", this prevents us from falling into an unhealthy victimhood trap. Although excruciatingly difficult at times, if we can somehow find acceptance and grace through life's trials and tribulations - our journey is made somewhat easier.

Fragile Awareness

All of our wisdom traditions and religions refer to this notion in some way – the idea that through pain and suffering, that somehow something more beautiful is created. We enter this world with a sense of incompleteness and we spend our entire lives trying to achieve a state of wholeness and happiness - yet ironically, these elevated states are very often achieved through difficult life-changing experiences, which force us to confront our pain, suffering, and the inevitable mortality we each share (Cain, 2022).

Stanford Psychology Professor, Laura Carstenson, has completed extensive research on adult life span development (Carstensen, 2000) and has noted that when people - both young and old, are more in touch with life's fragility, this increases their motivation to derive emotional meaning from life (Fung & Carstensen, 2006). Carstenson's research has demonstrated that when people develop an awareness of life's fragility - whether through natural aging or difficult circumstances that happen in youth - this leads to a shift in perspective, resulting in a greater urgency and appreciation of life's preciousness and fragility. Many of the wisdom traditions similarly teach that having an awareness of our own and others' mortality leads to deeper, more heart-felt connections - with less anger, more gratitude, and a focus on purposeful activities, and being in service to others (Cain, 2022).

The Bittersweet Cycle of Life

When my father passed in November 2016, it was my first close shave with the death of a loved one. Professionally, I had witnessed the effects of bereavement and loss, and had supported people on many occasions through grief - however, I felt somewhat inept at dealing with what

#DrDee

remained as yet, a conceptual term. I understood the expected stages and associated feelings of grief, however I hadn't myself fully experienced the deep and powerful significance of loss and grief on a personal level.

Historically, psychological research purported 'The Grief Work Hypothesis' as a necessary and systematic stage process for "working through" or adjusting to grief. This was later debunked in favour of the idea that everyone has their own unique way of processing and dealing with bereavement and loss, and no one way is superior ((Stroebe, 1993). In my case, although my Dad hadn't been in the best of health for some time, his death nevertheless came as a sudden, sobering shock. The sense of overwhelm, fear, sadness, disbelief, and piercing heartache are something I'll never forget.

Despite many tears, I slowly found my way, gaining solace in much of what he enjoyed – music, books, rugby, old photos, conversation, laughter and fun. I also immersed myself in what I knew worked from previous personal history worked, when I was feeling overwhelmed – exercise, meditation, reading, fashion and creativity, journaling and prayer - essentially anything that permitted me to connect with the freedom and beauty of emotional expression, whilst being reminded of my Dad along the way. In so doing, I was reminded of the bittersweet cycle of life and the juxtaposing emotions we often experience - which renewed my appreciation for all things living, as well as all things lost.

Death and Loss

Death takes us all in the end. We know this, yet somehow it still boggles the mind and takes us by surprise. We struggle to hold on, we struggle to let go. We forget that our time here is borrowed – a detail of which we're acutely reminded when death comes knocking. Rather than viewing death as a morbid contemplation therefore, if we use this knowledge as a reminder to live more fully, more passionately, more presently and with more grace, accepting life on life's terms - perhaps we might live with greater awareness, intent, compassion and integrity.

In her masterful work, 'Bittersweet: How Sorrow and Longing Make Us Whole', bestselling Author and Lecturer, Susan Cain proposes that bitter and sweet, light and dark, birth and death, are forever paired, and that contrary to modern thinking, our obsession with happiness is not making us happy, healthy or whole. Cain purports that it is only by embracing our darker emotions, as well as the light, that we discover our deepest meaning, connection, love, and joy. Together with Research Scientist and Johns Hopkins University Professor, Dr. David Yaden, and Cognitive Scientist and Author, Dr. Scott Barry Kaufman, Cain developed a 3 minute 'Bittersweet Quiz', which demonstrates how prone people are to these states of bitter-sweetness (freely available in her book and website).

Cain, Yaden & Kaufman's exploratory research findings, revealed that people who are high in bitter-sweetness, i.e. they can access states of both sadness and joy, demonstrate high levels of awe, wonder and spirituality. Their findings also revealed that those who scored high in bitter-sweetness tend to be more open and receptive to everything life brings, since they possess the ability to access all emotional states as opposed to becoming stuck on one, e.g. only being receptive to sadness, or only being comfortable in joy (Cain, 2022).

Psychology, defined and combined

Psychology is defined as the scientific study of human behaviour. As a professional Psychologist, I value and uphold science and research as being absolutely necessary informants to best practice, and to increasing the database of knowledge to the wider collective. I'm also aware that as an inexact science, not all human consciousness and behaviour can be objectively or statistically explained however - which is where Psychology uses probability theory to interpret empirical research findings.

It is my belief that science combined with intuition, offers a superior wealth of information - and that by combining the influence of both, we can view things from a more landscape perspective, as opposed to adopting spotlight consciousness solely. In addition to the application of formal, analytical, objective reasoning therefore, I believe intuition offers the extra emotional intelligence required to effectively read a situation, and make good decisions on the back of this.

The Science and Power of Intuition

According to the Oxford Dictionary, intuition is the ability to understand something instinctively, without the need for conscious reasoning. It is the spontaneous gut feeling, that bridges the gap between the conscious and unconscious mind. Intuition therefore, is our ability to know and understand something without formal analytic reasoning. When used in combination with objective, observable intelligence, intuition adds the magic ingredient essential to good decision making and successful outcomes. Dr. Judith Orloff, Medical Doctor and Assistant Clinical Professor of Psychiatry at UCLA, leads workshops on the relationships between medicine, intuition and spirituality, and has taken part in what she refers to as, 'intuitive research projects' (Weinstein, 2013). According to Dr. Orloff, scientists propose intuition operates through the entire right side of our brain - the brain's hippocampus, and through our gut, as the digestive system has neurons also (Orloff, 2001).

Spirituality

Often co-existing with intuition - though not exclusively so, is spirituality. Each person reading this will have their own understanding of what constitutes spirituality, and who's to say what opinion, practice or non-practice is any more valid than the next if it works for someone and allows them to lead a full and meaningful life? For me, spirituality includes respectfully holding space for everyone with whom I come into contact - regardless of how much their spiritual beliefs differ from mine. Whilst some may view spirituality as being directly connected to the soul, divine intelligence, source energy, the universe, the light, higher self, higher power, higher consciousness, nature or God - others may view it as being the same as religion and perhaps see it as oppressive, threatening, marginalising or punishing.

Spirituality for me, has God rocking front and centre stage, and far from being in any way oppressive or threatening, this powerful presence has enabled me considerably in my journey throughout life. I believe we are each unique expressions of the divine, and that we're guided by this higher intelligence to evolve and become the highest expressions of who we were created to be.

Noticing the Signs

Like spirituality, signs are something we either notice, or consider complete hogwash - and for those in the latter school of thought, this section may be of less interest. I believe signs, serendipities, and signals are divine messages sent to us from above, and it is within our gift regarding how we choose to read and interpret them. On any given day, we can either lean into the small still voice within, which is freely offered to us by spirit, or we can choose to steer our own ship. Whatever the case, I'm not here to convince you otherwise. I can only speak from my own experience, which is that I communicate with God, my Dad and the entire angelic realm on the daily, and I believe this offers me a steady and powerful source of guidance, wisdom and protection.

Like himself, my Dad communicates in vibrant, colourful ways. A firm favourite is the double rainbow - thought to be symbolic of spirit and other more subtle dimensions of consciousness. In ancient mythology, the double rainbow was seen to represent a bridge between heaven and earth. Other signs sent my way, include white feathers, songs, poetry, butterflies and particular sayings which were unique to him. In the past year, whilst my Mum has suffered poor physical health, I've spent quite a bit of time in our family home. She finds it comical hearing my interpretations of my Dad making his presence known to her with various signs - which have included a precocious blackbird who has relentlessly visited our back garden almost every day since his passing; an orange butterfly who majestically perches on her shoulder from time-to-time, and a little robin who occasionally stops by to say Hi also. Despite my best efforts to convince Maureen (my Mum) that these are Derry's special guest appearances - she remains curiously sceptical. However, it gives her

PSYCHOLOGY WITH A SPARKLE

a laugh in any event, to even contemplate the idea of Daddy keeping a watchful eye! Recently she made me laugh when she commented, "Sure he probably has nothing else to do"!

Rubbish or Real?

Whilst I appreciate this may be all too "kumbaya" or "woo-woo" for some, I believe there is much to be gained from considering the world of science, logic, and reason on the one hand, and the non-physical, timeless and incomprehensible on the other. I'm not here to convince anyone however, rather to share my personal belief that beyond the world of timelines, agendas, schedules and plans, there exists a magical realm of love, light and ethereal beauty. Often when I have ticked all the obvious boxes, and I'm still stuck or unsure about how to proceed with something, I'll ask for help and guidance from beyond. Although the insight may not appear immediately, something will invariably follow which I instinctively know is connected to my query. Even with regard to this book, my Dad was a voracious reader and gifted writer. Despite occasionally remarking, "I must write a book", it never came to pass, and although I scarcely hold a candle to his writing ability, I've felt his distinct presence the whole time throughout this writing journey - willing me forward, gently guiding me along the way.

Open Mind, Open Heart

When we're open to signs, synchronicities and serendipities, we experience them. If not, we put such moments down to chance or coincidence. Over the years, I have also consulted my share of psychics, mediums and intuitives - some of whom I occasionally speak with to this day, and whilst each have their own particular way of tapping into the magic and wisdom of spirit - more significantly, they inspire confidence in trusting our own inner guidance system, and committing to the path of personal responsibility and continued self-awareness.

| 126 |

#DrDee

> **"The heart knows in silence the secrets of the days and the nights, but the ears thirst for the sound of the heart's knowledge"**
> **– Khalil Gibran.**

Silence, prayer, meditation and connecting to nature, are among the reflective practices that enable the voice of the heart - most closely aligned to Spirit, God, or Divine Intelligence to be heard. Heart Consciousness provides the purest, most authentic feedback, allowing the mind to be purified so we can more easily recognise the ego. Through conscious, repetitive practice, we develop a greater connection between our emotional (reactional) brain and cognitive (thinking) brain - resulting in clearer, more conscious thought, as well as more heart-felt, discerning choices and decision making.

When searching for answers, one thing we can be sure, is that the voice of Spirit, Higher Power, Nature or God, is never loud, brash, impatient, unjust or unkind. It doesn't seek to hurt, humiliate, separate or offend - as is often the case with the ego. Once we are connected to and making choices from the heart space, we generally make less errors in judgment, and our ability to communicate in a kind, compassionate manner is greatly enhanced. This is not to say we are entirely saved from our earthly, reactive natures. As humans, we will still experience our nervous systems becoming activated and triggered at certain times and with certain people. However, through repeated, mindful practice, we become better able to recognise the voice of spirit as distinct from the voice of the ego, and we can more easily respond from that calm, centred place.

Faith under Fire

Like many, my faith has been tested over the years. I question why good people so often experience pain, loss, abandonment, suffering, poverty, crime, war, discrimination, racism, inequality, cruelty, abuse, neglect, hunger, exclusion, isolation – to name a few. This remains one of life's mysteries and we can only ever do our part in whatever small way, to alleviate suffering and be of service to others. Life indiscriminately and relentlessly presents challenge to each of us – our health fails, someone we love receives a life-threatening diagnosis, we struggle to conceive, we don't get the job, the relationship doesn't work out, we're bullied, undermined, we lose someone we love, our friend betrays us, our partner is unfaithful, our child is battling a serious illness, our business goes downhill. Life's persistent stream of challenges escapes no one.

During these times, it's normal to feel anger, sadness, resentment, disappointment, guilt, hurt, jealousy, rage, regret. All emotion comes to teach us something - and in the case of emotions we perceive as negative, they may be signalling a reminder to examine something on a deeper level, and to order our steps accordingly. Feeling anxious? Maybe we need to tackle that task we've been avoiding. Feeling lonely? Maybe we need to reach out and connect with someone. Feeling excluded? Maybe we need to channel our energy into someone or something that feels more restorative. Feeling guilty? Maybe we need to journal, apologise or let go. Feeling resentful? Perhaps we need to meditate or seek therapeutic support. Feeling angry? Maybe we need to speak to the person with whom we feel aggrieved, or explore the anger therapeutically. Feeling jealous? Maybe we may need to examine what goals or unfulfilled ambitions are being triggered by the other. Feeling lethargic? Maybe we need some fresh air, exercise and/or sleep. Feeling unloved? Maybe we need to extend ourselves more self-love or learn to open our hearts to others more. Feeling bored or helpless? Maybe we can volunteer to be of service to others. Feeling victimised? Perhaps we need to take personal responsibility and reclaim our authentic power.

Rather than repressing difficult emotions, we fare better by giving them the required air time and acknowledgment they deserve. In the words of Pema Chodron, "Nothing ever goes away until it has taught us what we need to know."

Faith, Purpose and Belief

Having faith and belief in a power greater than myself, whom I choose to call God, has allowed me to navigate life, however imperfectly - with optimism, compassion, courage, enthusiasm and humour. On a daily basis, I ask for guidance in everything - from the minutiae details of my day, to the more complex. I ask for support regarding my health, personal relationships, fitness, finances, food related choices and personal goals. Similarly, I ask for guidance regarding my work and how to best support and be of service to my clients, co-workers, supervisors, supervisees and extended professionals alike. Whilst I don't always get it right – I mess up, make mistakes and get triggered just like every other human - however, I believe if we're well intentioned and approach things from a heart-centred space, as well as from the intellect, we're less likely to wander too far off course - and if and when we do, we have the ability to course-correct at an earlier stage.

Embrace you

Over the years, my Mum has always affectionately referred to me as being "different", relaying how much I remind her of my Dad. This is something I've always taken pride in, as I believe that whilst we each have a shared human connection with many similar desires and experiences, it's important we celebrate our uniqueness and what we bring to the world - not feeling compelled to follow the crowd. I procrastinated for so long about writing this book, which I knew didn't perhaps conform to traditional orthodox psychology standards (certainly not this chapter) - yet my gut told me to press ahead regardless. The needle needs to be moved and grooved in most, if not all professions - and whilst I'm not suggesting we all become spiritual enthusiasts, it's important we're unafraid of marking our true expression in the world.

Wherever you are and whatever your beliefs, one of the best things you can do for yourself and others, is to whole-heartedly accept, embrace and embody your multi-dimensional, unique and wonderful self! What we hold shame about, can neither be healed nor celebrated - so fly your colours with confidence, freedom, pride and grace, and leave room in your heart for a little weirdness, awkwardness, and imperfection. In so doing, you'll give others permission to do the same. So many people go through life hiding their particular talents, gifts, feelings, flaws, thoughts, quirks, facts and fetishes - for fear of being judged, shamed, shunned or criticised. But the world would be very boring if we were all the same, surely?

'Follow your arrow wherever it points'
- Kacey Musgraves

Final Thoughts

1) Accept the moment as though you have chosen it. However difficult this moment is, try not to resist it as this will create further tension and discord.
2) The Universe will always reflect back the energy we are putting out, so align yourself with what you most want to receive.
3) In order to evolve to our highest potential, it's important to retain a mind-set of learning, growth and gratitude, so that this frequency becomes our point of attraction. A simple way to short circuit this process is to ask ourselves, "How can I best serve?" as opposed to "What can I get?"
4) Be satisfied and practice deep gratitude for what is, whilst aspiring toward dreams and goals. We cannot expect to receive more if we do not appreciate what we already have.
5) Energy goes where attention flows. Whatever we put our energy into will grow and flourish, and what we take our attention away from, will recede and eventually diminish.
6) Recognise the power of thoughts in creating who and what you become. Our physical lives very often reflect our thought lives.
7) Inspire others by doing what you love. The more joy we embody, the more powerful and potent our energy, which enhances our ability to inspire, positively influence and best serve those around us.
8) Be happy for others and recognise that there is room for everyone. In the words of International Author and Speaker, Russel Brand, "Envy is your own unrealised potential projected onto another". No amount of envy or jealousy will get you any closer to your goal, so when you see others who have what you want - be happy

for them. Release the energy of comparison and jealousy, and instead see their situation as a source of inspiration toward your own dream activation. Believe that similar success is attainable for you if you work for it, and it's aligned with your higher purpose.

9) If something doesn't work out, trust that it wasn't meant for you and that something better is on its way. In so doing, fear and rejection occupy less space in our minds, enabling a more joyful, optimistic attitude to take further inspired action.

10) When we are aligned with God, The Divine, Spirit, The Universe, Higher Consciousness, or however we choose to identify with the Source of all Creation - perception of lack fades. We know and trust that each one of us comes with a specific mission, dharma or life-purpose, which relates to how we are designed to best serve and contribute to the world.

11) What is destined to be yours will never pass you by, so stay in your own power, release fear and attachment to the outcome, and continue giving the world your best - whilst accepting life as it unfolds.

12) Stay connected to God or however you choose to identify with the Source of all Creation. Ask for guidance in all matters concerning your life and listen closely as your inner GPS navigates and directs your path.

13) According to International Author, Speaker and Manifestation Coach, Gabrielle Bernstein, the key to manifesting is feeling good. By identifying the negative thoughts that hold us back from feeling good, we become more aware of the deeply held belief systems that often lie behind negative thought patterns and block our manifestations from occurring. Working with someone therapeutically, may help with identifying negative automatic thoughts, as well as beliefs and behaviour patterns - whilst offering tools for dealing with each.

14) When manifesting desires, the teachings of mystical Author Neville Goddard, recommends affirming our wish, visualising the end result of how it will look and feel when the goal is achieved, continuing to take inspired daily action and releasing our attachment to the outcome.

#DrDee

15) Never take yourself or others too seriously. Life is short so make time for the people and things that bring you joy and keep your sense of humour!

16) Give freely in time and spirit to others. Individual success, self-driven ambitions contribute to happiness, though rarely offer the joy and contentment of being of genuine service to others.

17) Shine brightly, courageously and daringly!

"This place where you are right now,
God circled on a map for you."
- Hafiz

REFERENCES AND BIBLIOGRAPHY

Ainsworth, Mary D. et al. (2015) Patterns of Attachment. Taylor & Francis Ltd. U.K.

Allen, James (2007) As a Man Thinketh. Dover Publications Inc, U.S.

Amen, Daniel, G. (2009) The Brain in Love. Random House, U.S.

Amen, Daniel, G. (2018) Feel Better Fast and Make It Last. Tyndale House Publishers, U.S.

Amen, Daniel, G. (2015) Change Your Brain, Change Your Life. Potter/Harmony U.S.

Instagram: @doc_amen Podcast: The Brain Warriors Way Podcast

Arnheim, Rudolf (1979) in Leaf, Caroline (2010) The Gift in You. Improv Limited, U.S.

Aurelius, Marcus: "Our life is what our thoughts make it." google.com

Ban Breathnach, Sarah (1997) Simple Abundance: A Daybook of Comfort & Joy. Transworld Publishers Ltd. U.K.

Beck, Aaron (1967) Cognitive Behaviour Therapy

Bernstein, Gabrielle (2018) Judgment Detox. Hay House, U.K.

Bernstein, Gabrielle (2021) Super Attractor. Hay House, U.K.

Bernstein, Gabrielle (2016) The Universe Has Your Back. Hay House, U.K.

Instagram: @gabbybernstein Podcast: Dear Gabby

Bowlby, John (1997) Attachment. Vintage, U.K.

Brand, Russel (2018) Recovery: Freedom from our Addictions. Pan MacMillan, U.K.

Instagram: @russellbrand Podcast: Under the Skin

Bransby, Thomas (2018) Lost Connections: Uncovering the Real Causes of Depression – and the Unexpected Solutions. British Journal of General Practice 2018; 68 (672):331

Brown, Brene (2015) Daring Greatly: How the Courage to be Vulnerable Transforms the Way We Live, Love, Parent and Lead. Penguin Books Ltd. UK

Brown, Brene (2019) The Call to Courage, Netflix Documentary

Brown, Brene; Instagram @brenebrown

Buddha: *"Holding onto anger is like grasping a hot coal with the intent of throwing it at someone else; you are the one who gets burned"*. google.com

Buettner, Dan (2019) The Blue Zones of Happiness. National Geographic Society, U.S.

Bukoski, Charles: *"The problem with the world is that fools and fanatics are always so certain of themselves, yet wiser people are full of doubts."* google.com

Bush, Zach (2022) Instagram: Zach Bush, MD @zachbushmd

Byrne, Rhonda (2006) The Secret. Simon & Schuster, U.S.

Byrne, Rhonda (2012) The Magic. Simon & Schuster Ltd., U.K.

Byrne, Rhonda (2010) The Power. Simon & Schuster Ltd., U.K.

Byrne, Rhonda (2020) The Greatest Secret, Harper Collins Publishers, U.K.

Cain, Susan (2022) Bittersweet: How Sorrow and Longing Make Us Whole. Crown Publishing Group, U.S.

Cain, Susan; Yaden, David & Kaufman, Scott Barry (2022) Bittersweet Quiz; susancain.net

Cain, Susan TED Talk: The Hidden Power of sad songs and rainy days

Cain, Susan (2022) Turn Sadness into a Superpower and Find Wholeness in Your Life. EP 1287 Lewis Howes School of Greatness Podcast

Carnegie, Dale (2011) How to Stop Worrying and Start Living. Simon & Schuster, U.S.

Cassel, John (2017) Physical illness in response to stress. Social Stress, 189-209

Castensen, Laura; Pasupathi, Monisha; Mayr, Ulrich; Nesselroade, John (2000) Emotional experience in everyday life across the adult life span. Journal of Personality and Social Psychology, 79(4), 644

Chanel, Coco: "Before you leave the house, look in the mirror and take one thig off." Fashion Quotes, google.com

Chapman, Gary (2015) The 5 Love Languages, Moody Publishers, U.S.

Cherry, Kendra (2022) What is Attachment Theory? verywellmind.com

Chodron, Pema: *"Nothing ever goes away until it has taught up what we need to know."* google.com

Chopra, Deepak (2015) The Seven Spiritual Laws of Success. Amber-Allen Publishing, U.S.

Chopra, Deepak (2021) Ageless Body. Timeless Mind, Ebury Publishing, U.K.

Clear, James (2018) Atomic Habits. Random House Business Books, U.K.

Coelho, Paulo (2014) The Alchemist. Harper Collins Publishers Inc., U.S.

Coelho, Paulo (2011) Warrior of the Light. Harper, U.S.

Cohen, Leonard (1992) *"There is a crack in everything, that's how the light gets in"*. Anthem. Stranger Music Inc.

Copeland, Mary, E. (1997) Wellness Recovery Action Plan. Drummerston, VT: Peach Prress.
copelandcentre.com

Couelle, F. (2014) Attached: The New Science of Adult Attachment and How it can help you find and keep love by Amir Levine and Rachel Heller (2010), published by Jeremy P. Tarcher/Penguin. Attachment: New Directions in Relational Psychoanalysis and Psychotherapy 8 (1), 101-103

Covey, Stephen R. (2020) The 7 Habits of Highly Effective People. Simon & Schuster

Cuddy, Amy (2012) Your body language may shape who you are. Ted Talk, You Tube

Cuddy, Amy (2016) Presence: Bringing Your Boldest Self to your Biggest Challenges. Orion Publishing Co. U.K.

Dahl, Roald: *"If you have good thoughts, they will shine out of your face like sunbeams and you will always look lovely."* Good Quotes, google.com

De Mello, Anthony (1990) Awareness. Harper-Collins Publishers, U.K.

Dispenza, Joe (2013) Breaking the Habit of Being Yourself. Hay House, U.S.
Instagram: Dr. Joe Dispenza @drjoedispenza

Dispenza, Joe (2022) The School of Greatness Podcast with Lewis Howes, Ep. 1256
'Unlock the full potential of your Mind.'

Dolan-Leto, kim (2016) F.I.T. Faith Inspired Transformation. Newtype, U.S.

Dolan-Leto, Kim (2020) Strong, Confident, His: Faith & Fitness Devotional. U.S.

Instagram: @kimdolanleto Podcast: Strong, Confident, His

Donne, J. (1642) "No man is an island." Sermon by the Dean of St. Paul's Cathedral. google.com

Doty, James (2016) Into the Magic Shop. Hodder & Stoughton, U.K.

Dyer, Wayne (2012) Wishes Fulfilled. Hay House, U.K.

Dyer, Wayne (2009) Change Your Thoughts, Change Your Life. Hay House Inc. U.S.

Emerson, Ralph Waldo: *"A man is what he thinks about all day long, how could he be anything else."* google.com

Eriksson, G., Kottorp, A., Borg, J., Tham, K. (2009) Relationship between occupational gaps in everyday life, depressive mood and life satisfaction after acquired brain Injury. Journal of Rehabilitation Medicine 41(3), 187-194

Eurich, Tasha (2018) Insight: How to succeed by seeing yourself clearly. Pan Macmillan, U.K.

Fischer, Helen (2004) Why We Love. Henry Holt & Company, Australia

Fischer, Helen (2014) The brain in love. Ted Talk. google.com

Fischer, Helen (2014) Why we love, why we cheat. Ted Talk. google.com

Fung, Helene & Carstensen, Laura (2006) Goals change when life's fragility is primed: Lessons learned from older adults, the September attacks and sars. Social Cognition 24(3) 248-278

Helen Fischer Ted Talk, 'The Brain in Love'

Ford, Tom: *"You should put on the best version of yourself when you go out into the world, because it is a show of respect to the people around you."* Fashion Quotes, google.com

Frankl, Viktor, E. (2015) Man's Search For Meaning. Ebury Publishing, U.K.

Fraser, Cheryl (2019) Buddha's Bedroom. New Harbinger Publications, U.S.

Gibran, Khalil (2013) The Prophet, Benediction Classics, U.K.

Gilbert, Elizabeth (2007) Eat, Pray, Love. Bloomsbury Publishing PLC. U.K.

Gilbert, Elizabeth (2010) Committed: A Sceptic Makes Peace with Marriage. Bloomsbury Publishing PLC, U.K.

Gilbert, Elizabeth (2016) Big Magic. Bloomsbury Publishing PLC, UK

Godard, Jean Luc: *It is not where you take things from, it is where you take them to.*" Fashion Quotes, google.com

Goddard, Neville (2013) Feeling is the Secret. Merchant Books

Goddard, Neville (2015) The Secret of Imagining. Watchmaker Publishing

Google.com "The definition of insanity is doing the same thing over and over, and expecting a different result."

Growl, David: *"No one is you and that is your power."* google.com

Hafiz, Mohammad. *"This place where you are right now, God circled on a map for you."* Quoted by Author, Elizabeth Gilbert in her Super Soul Special with Oprah, "The Curiosity-Driven Life, 2019.

Hanson, Rick (2012) Buddha's Brain: The practical neuroscience of happiness, love & wisdom. New Harbinger Publications

Hanson, Rick (2015) Hardwiring Happiness. Ebury Publishing

Hari, Johann (2018) Lost Connections. Bloomsbury Publishing PLC

Hayes, Stephen; Strosahl, Kirk & Wilson, Kelly (2016) Acceptance and Commitment Therapy. The Guilford Press, U.S.

Hicks, Esther & Jerry (2004) Ask and it is Given. Hay House Inc., New York, U.S.

Howes, Lewis: Instagram: @lewishowes Podcast: The School of Greatness

Hubbard, Elbert: *"To avoid criticism, do nothing, say nothing, be nothing."* Hubbard Quotes, google.com

Innes, Jocasta: *"Food for the eye is to be found almost everywhere"*. In Ban Breathnach, Sarah (1997) Simple Abundance: A Daybook of Comfort & Joy. Transworld Publishers Ltd. U.K.

Jacobs, Marc: *"Let's do what we love and do a lot of it."* Fashion Quotes, google.com

James 2:14-26 *"Faith without works is dead."* BibleGateway.com

James, William (2000) The Principles of Psychology. Dover Publications Inc. U.S.

John, Elton: *"It was part of the ritual of performing. I couldn't wear jeans because I was too fat for jeans, but I had to get into costume, where there was an element of theatre, drama, occasion, performance."* You Tube

Jones, Kimberly (2020) Shut Hell Up. Charisma House, U.S. Instagram: @realtalkkim Podcast: Real Talk Kim

Jung, Carl, G. (2006) The Undiscovered Self. Penguin Putnam Inc, U.S.

Kaufman, Scott Barry; Yaden, David et al. (2019) The light vs. dark triad of personality: Contrasting two very different profiles of human nature. Frontiers in Psychology 10, 467

Keighin, M; Butcher, K; Darnell, M. (2009) The effect of introversion and extroversion on the fear of negative evaluation. Undergraduate Research Journal for the Human Sciences 8 (1).

Kondo, Marie: *"Discard anything that does not spark joy."* Marie Kondo Quotes, google.com

Lacroix, Christian: *"Elegance is not to pass unnoticed, but to get to the very soul of who one is."* In Ban Breathnach, Sarah (1997) Simple Abundance: A Daybook of Comfort & Joy. Transworld Publishers Ltd. U.K.

Lagerfeld, Karl: *"A respectable appearance is sufficient to make people more interested in your appearance."* Fashion Quotes, google.com

LaPorte, Danielle (2014) The Desire Map. Sounds True Inc. U.S. Instagram: @daniellelaporte

Leaf, Caroline (2015) Switch On Your Brain. Baker Publishing Group, U.S.

Leaf, Caroline (2021) Lewis Howes' School of Greatness Podcast

Leaf, Caroline (2010) The Gift in You. Improv Limited, U.S.

Leaf, Caroline (2021) Your Mental Mess. Baker Publishing Group, U.S.

Lefebvre, Henri: *"But let's not forget, fashion is a game: getting dressed up is wanting to play."* Fashion Quotes, google.com

Lehrer, Paul, M; Woolfolk, Robert L. (2021) Principles and Practice of Stress Management. The Guilford Press, U.S.

LePera, Nicole (2021) How To Do The Work. Harper-Collins Publishers Inc. U.S. Instagram: @the.holistic.psychologist

Levine, Amir & Heller, Rachel S. (2019) Attached. Pan MacMillan, U.K.

Levy, Terry (2021) The Dependency Paradox in Relationships. Evergreen Psychotherapy Centre, May 2021. Attachment, Theory & Research

Luskin, Fred (2012) cited in Comaford, Christine (2012) Got Inner Peace? 5 Ways to Get It Now. forbes.com

Mallaya, S., Sutherland, J., Pongracic, S. (2015) The manifestation of Anxiety Disorders after traumatic brain injury: a review. Journal of Neurotrauma 32(7), 411-421

Maloof, Molly (2022) Aubrey Marcus Podcast with Dr. Molly Maloof
Instagram: @aubreymarcus @drmolly.co

Maslow, Abraham (1943) 'A Theory of Human Motivation', The Journal of Psychological Review

Maslow, Abraham (2015) Maslow's Hierarchy of Needs, 50minutes.com

Maté, Gabriel with Daniel Maté (2022) The Myth of Normal. Trauma, Illness and Healing in a Toxic Culture. Ebury Publishing, U.K.

Maté, Gabriel (2019) When the Body Says No. Ebury Publishing, U.K.

Matthew 5:45 *"The rain falls on the just and the unjust."* biblegateway.com via Instagram @realtalkkim

Matthew 22:12 The wedding parable bibletools.org

McConaughey, Mathew (2020) Greenlights. Headline Publishing Group, U.K.

Monroe, Marilyn (1953) "It's not true that I had nothing on, I had the radio on." quoteinvestigator.com

Morse, Emily: Instagram @sexwithemily Podcast: Sex with Emily

Muise, Amy; Schimmack, Ulrich; Impett, Emily A. (2016) Sexual frequency predicts greater wellbeing, but more is not always better. Social Psychological and Personality Science 7 (4) 295-302

Murphy, Robyn (2020) Your Genes are not Your Destiny: A Guide to Epigenetics. Part 1. aor.ca

Musgraves, Kacey (2013) Song: Follow Your Arrow; Album: Same Trailer Different Park. Song written by Musgraves, Brandy Clark and Shane McAnally

O'Dwyer, Denise (2015) #TwentyFirstCenturyRecovery: Examining Wellness Recovery Action Planning (WRAP) within the contexts of Acquired Brain Injury and Adult Mental Health. Post Chartered Doctoral Research, City University, London.

Orloff, Judith (2001) Dr. Judith Orloff's Guide To Intuitive Health. Random House USA Inc. U.S.

Osteen, Joel (2015) The Power of I Am. John Murray Press, U.K.

Osteen, Joel (2014) You Can, You Will. Time Warner Trade Publishing, U.S.

Osteen, Joel (2012) I Declare. Grand Central Publishing, U.S.
Instagram: @joelosteen Podcast: Joel Osteen Daily Podcast

Perel, Esther (2007) Mating in Captivity. Hodder & Stoughton, U.K.

Perel, Esther (2018) The State of Affairs. Harper Paperbacks, U.K.
Insta: @estherperelofficial Podcast: Where Should We Begin with Esther Perel
Perlmutter, David (2019) in Amen, Daniel (2020) The End of Mental Illness. Tyndale House Publishers, U.S.
Peters, Steve (2012) The Chimp Paradox. Ebury Press, U.K.
Proverbs 23:7 *"As a man thinketh in his heart, so is he."* BibleGateway.com
Rickman, C (2012) Research by Dr. Fred Luskin of Stanford University. Cited in 'The Digital Business Start-Up Workbook: The Ultimate Step-by-step Guide to succeeding online'. scholar.google.com
Rindfuss, Bryan (2009) Arts: What ought to wear, San Antonio Current Sacurrent.com
Robbins, Anthony (1986) Unlimited Power. Fawcett Columbine, U.S.
Robbins, Anthony (2001) Awaken the Giant Within. Simon & Schuster, U.K.
Robertson, Ian (2021) How Confidence Works. Transworld Publishers Ltd.
Rohn, Jim (2013) The Philosophy for Successful Living. No Dream Too Big LLC.
Roosevelt, Eleanor: "Comparison is the thief of joy." Eleanor Roosevelt Quotes, google.com
Ruiz, Don, M. (1997) The Four Agreements. Amber-Allen Publishing, U.S.
Rumi (2013) Rumi's little Book of Life: The Garden of the Soul, the Heart and the Spirit. Translated by Azima MelitaKolin, Maryam Mafi
Sandberg, C. (2015) Lean In. Ebury Publishing, U.K.
Santos, Laurie (2021) Podcast: The Happiness Lab with Dr. Laurie Santos
Seligman, Martin (2004) Authentic Happiness. Simon & Schuster, U.K.
Seligman, Martin (2006) Learned Optimism. Random House, U.S.
Shakespeare, William: *"Nothing is ever good or bad, but thinking makes it so."* – from 'Hamlet'.
Shakespeare, William: *"All the world is a stage, and the men and women merely players."* – from 'As You Like It'.
Sharma, Robin (2011) The Monk who sold his Ferrari. Harper Collins Publishers, U.K.
Sharma, Robin (2018) The 5 A.M. Club. Harper Collins Publishers, U.K.

Shetty, Jay (2020) Think Like A Monk. Harper-Collins Publishers, U.K. Instagram: @jayshetty Podcast: On Purpose with Jay Shetty

Shetty, Jay (2020) Lewis Howes' School of Greatness Podcast, Ep. 1003 'Mindset Habits for Happiness and Thinking Like a Monk.'

Spencer, Diana (1993) YouTube: Princess Diana's Speech on Eating Disorders

Steinbeck, John (Jan 1st, 1941) in A Life in Letters (2001) Penguin Classics, U.K.

Stroebe, Margaret (1993) Coping with bereavement: A review of the grief work hypothesis. OMEGA Journal of Death and Dying, 26(1), 19-42

Thoits, Peggy A (2011) Mechanisms linking social ties and support to physical and mental health. Journal of Health and Social Behaviour, 145-161

Tolle, Eckhart (2004) The Power of Now. Universe Publishing, U.S.

Tolle, Eckhart (2011) A New Earth. Penguin Putnam Inc., U.S. Instagram: @eckharttolle Podcast: Eckhart Tolle Essential Teachings

Ury, Logan (2021) How To Not Die Alone. Little, Brown Book Group, U.K.

Vaynerchuk, Gary (2020) *"Social media is not responsible for making people develop entitled attitudes, it has simply heightened people's predispositions to becoming that way"*. The Garyvee Audio Experience Podcast. Instagram: Gary Vay-Ner-Chuk @garyvee

Von Furstenberg, Diane: *"Style is something each of us already has, we just need to find it."* Fashion Quotes, google.com

Vreeland, Diana: *"The only real elegance is in the mind; if you have that, the rest really comes from there."* In Ban Breathnach, Sarah (1997) Simple Abundance: A Daybook of Comfort and Joy. Transworld Publishers Ltd., U.K.

Wagner, M. & Morisi, D. (2019) Anxiety, fear, and political decision making. Oxford research encyclopaedia of politics. wagnermarkus.net

Wason, Peter (1960) Confirmation bias

Weinstein, Edie (2013) Second Sight: An Interview with Dr. Judith Orloff, Wisdom magazine, Jan 11th, 2013

Weir, Kirsten (2012) The pain of social rejection. Vol 43. No. 4 American Psychological Association apa.org

Wilde, Oscar: *"Be yourself, everyone else is already taken."*
"It is only shallow people who do not judge by appearances." google.com
Williamson, Marianne (2011) A Return to Love. Harper-Collins Publishers Inc., U.S.
Williamson, Marianne (2001) Enchanted Love. Simon & Schuster, Australia
Williamson, Marianne (2016) A Year of Miracles. Harper-Collins Publishers Inc., U.S.
Windeman, C; McCurdy, A.; Lamboglia, C.G.; Wohlers, B. (2020) The extent to which family physicians record their patients' exercise in medical records: a scoping review. British Medical Journal open 2020 bmjopen.bmj.com
Winfrey, Oprah & Perry, Bruce D (2021) What Happened To You. Pan MacMillan, U.K.
Winfrey, Oprah (2015) What I know for sure. Pan MacMillan, U.K.
Winfrey, Oprah (2019) The Path Made Clear. Pan MacMillan, U.K.
Wordsworth, William: *"To begin, begin."* Wordsworth Quotes, google.com
Yaden, David & Kaufman, Scott Barry (2022) Bittersweet Quiz. susancain.net
Yaden, David; Kaufman, Scott Barry et al (2019) The development of Awe Experience Scale (AWE-S); A multifactorial measure for a complex emotion. The Journal of Positive Psychology 14(4), 474-488
Yeats, William, Butler: *"Think where man's glory begins and ends, and say, my glory was I had such friends."* Yeats Quotes, google.com
Yves Saint Laurent: *"Fashions fade, style is eternal."* Fashion Quotes, google.com
Zoe, Rachel: *"Clothes are a way of saying who we are, without having to speak."* Fashion Quotes, google.com
Zukav, Gary (1991) The Seat of the Soul, Ebury Publishing, U.K.

APPENDICES

Mean values for Pre and Post measures of the Hospital & Anxiety Depression Scale (HADS). HADS anxiety, HADS depression and the Wellness Recovery Action Planning (WRAP) scales, are shown in Table 1 below:

GROUP		HADS anxiety pre	HADS anxiety post	HADS depression pre	HADS depression post	WRAP pre	WRAP post
ABI intervention	Mean	9.36	6.69	6.83	5.20	8.03	4.33
	N	22	29	29	30	30	30
	Std. Deviation	2.85	3.33	2.83	2.72	3.72	5.13
	Kurtosis	-.62	.13	.22	.72	-.92	-.24
	Std. Error of Kurtosis	.95	.85	.85	.83	.83	.83
	Skewness	.24	.64	.42	.28	-.36	1.16
	Std. Error of Skewness	.49	.43	.43	.43	.43	.43
ABI control	Mean	7.88	8.29	7.24	7.47	4.94	4.82
	N	17	17	17	17	17	17
	Std. Deviation	3.28	3.22	4.21	3.86	3.78	3.30
	Kurtosis	-.01	.90	-1.17	-.94	-2.06	-2.05
	Std. Error of Kurtosis	1.06	1.06	1.06	1.06	1.06	1.06
	Skewness	-.26	-.07	.07	.32	-.15	.07
	Std. Error of Skewness	.55	.55	.55	.55	.55	.55
MH intervention	Mean	11.52	7.77	8.64	5.24	6.07	1.74
	N	27	26	22	21	27	27
	Std. Deviation	5.47	4.17	5.44	4.05	2.11	2.60
	Kurtosis	-1.03	3.18	-.90	4.49	.93	4.15
	Std. Error of Kurtosis	.87	.89	.95	.97	.87	.87
	Skewness	.34	1.11	.48	1.85	-.87	2.15
	Std. Error of Skewness	.45	.46	.49	.50	.45	.45

#DrDee

MH control	Mean	10.77	11.13	7.29	8.10	4.83	4.98
	N	31	31	31	29	29	31
	Std. Deviation	5.33	5.21	4.33	5.10	3.33	3.48
	Kurtosis	-.70	-.66	-.58	-.90	.05	-1.08
	Std. Error of Kurtosis	.82	.82	.82	.85	.85	.82
	Skewness	-.39	-.35	.08	.24	.55	.03
	Std. Error of Skewness	.42	.42	.42	.43	.43	.42
Total	Mean	10.15	8.56	7.44	6.47	6.11	3.93
	N	97	103	99	97	103	105
	Std. Deviation	4.72	4.48	4.21	4.19	3.48	3.99
	Kurtosis	-.31	-.01	-.14	.30	-.69	-.02
	Std. Error of Kurtosis	.49	.47	.48	.49	.47	.47
	Skewness	.27	.52	.47	.83	.04	.98
	Std. Error of Skewness	.25	.24	.24	.25	.24	.24

TABLE 1: Means and Distributional Statistics for HADS and WRAP Measures

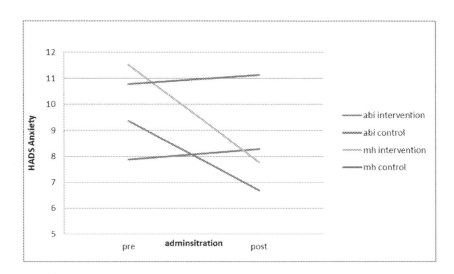

FIGURE 1: HADS Anxiety means for each group at time 1 (before) and time 2 (after)

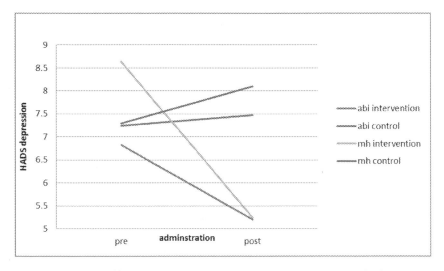

FIGURE 2: HADS Depression Means for each group at time 1 (before) and time 2 (after)

#DrDee

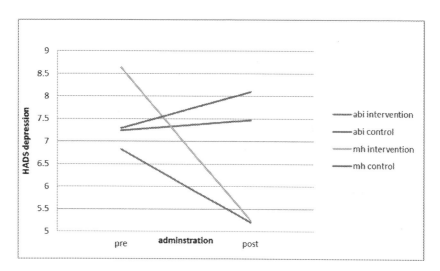

Figure 3: WRAP means for each group at time 1 (before) and time 2 (after)

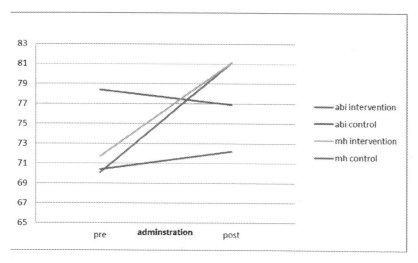

Figure 4: MHRM scores pre and post intervention for ABI and Mental Health Intervention and Control Groups

Thank you for sharing this journey with me,

Keep Sparkling!

Dr Dee X

Printed in the United States
by Baker & Taylor Publisher Services